Heaven's

Special

Mum

LORRAINE TOWNSEND

Heaven's Special Mum

Heaven's Special Mum

ISBN 9780992415105

Acknowledgements - Prologue

I realized almost too late most of the people had gone who could answer my questions, the only parent I had left was my dad and he was getting old too, so I asked him to tell me about his life.

With a cassette recorder set on the table a cup of tea in hand Dad began recalling his earliest childhood memories, rolling through the years to how he had meet mum (Beryl Wyber) and the life they shared together.

Merging the information, as well with my research work, slowly like a jigsaw-puzzle bit by bit the pieces came together recapturing those years.

Heaven's Special Mum

Credit Page Home

Many thanks are given to ….To my family –

My husband: Gary Townsend who has taken the journey with me.

My father: Reg Rae, who took the time to tell me his story.

Grandmother: Annie Burkhardt   the keeper of our family tree 1902-1981

Aunt: Dot Pedersen for keeping the treasured memories safe 1925-1996

Aunt: Nancye Wyber

Aunt: Dot O' Neill,

Cousin: Bert Guest

Cousin: Robyn Foye

Cousin: Barbra Quinn,

Cousin: Ron Wyber & his wife Charlotte

Second Cousin: Kate Quinn.

Contents

Heaven's Special Mum

Chapter 1

And so the story of my mother's life begins..........

Vavau was an enchanting late Victorian style period house, located in Park Road Sydney in the suburb of Auburn. The three chimney house had a slate tiled hip and valley roof, decorated with combination trim and gable post. The rendered brick-work was painted light cream. The front of the L shaped house had triple arched bay windows, ornamentally enhanced with plaster décor mouldings.

The surrounding veranda, sheltered by an awning of alternate maroon and white corrugated iron roofing, is edged with wrought-iron-lace painted white. Adding to its charm, the house was hedged with Roses in various shades of colour, both climbing and Old World. Once a private dwelling it was now converted into a Private Maternity Hospital.

On 26th October 1927 it was spring, a time of rebirth, renewal and regrowth. In this place and at this time, Beryl was the third child born to William and Annie Wyber; she has a half-brother William Jr. aged 16, Robert aged 4 and a sister Dorothy aged 2.

In the year she was born so too was the first talking motion picture, called 'The Jazz Singer'... Starring Al Jolson singing the songs that made him famous...

♫'Toot toot tootsie! Good bye'
♫'Blue Sky's'
♫'Mammy Mammy'

"Vavau" Private Maternity

The Fashions of the day

Beryl's father William was born in 1889 and came from Newcastle-on-Tyne, England. He was the sixth child of eleven children, four girls and seven boys born to parents Adamson and Margaret Wyber (nee Curtis) and like his father worked for The St Lawrence Ironworks, where he had completed his apprenticeship as a Plater.

In 1913 William was a brilliant Sydney forward, who had been chosen to represent the English-born in the International fixtures at Epping and was known to all Football enthusiasts as 'William the Wizard.'[1]

In 1920 he played for Canterbury Senior Soccer Club Sydney NSW.[2] In 1927 when Beryl arrived he was 39-years-old and his Soccer days were over.

---

[1] The Sydney Morning Herald Monday 29 September 1913 p 7

[2] The Sydney Morning Herald Monday 31 May 1920 p 11

~Canterbury Senior Soccer Football Club- 1921~

Top line: T. Brown, (Vice Pres) V. H. Willingale (Hon. Sec) W. Griffiths, H. Wright (Vice Pres) B. Freckleton, L. Gallagher (Vic Pres) A.J. Lane (Assist. Hon. Sec)

Second line from top: L. Lander, A. C. Griffiths, H. Ogden (Trainer), T. Forbes, D. McLennan, R. H. Midgley (President) A. Forbes, (Vice Captain) C. Lander, R. White, J. Cornell.

Third line tops: W. Wyber, G. Barton, F. Fortier (Captain) G. Dean. L. Hippisley. Bottom line: J. Shepley, L. Coley, P. Stafford, H. Bastock (absent) (Trainer)

Portrait Commissioned
6ᵗʰ August 1926
William Wyber 37

Annie Wyber

William Wyber's passbook description: Height 5ft 4¾ inches, eyes brown, long nose, small mouth, round chin, brown hair with a fair coloured oval face.

In the 1st World War, William was awarded the British War Medal and the Victory Medal while serving in the Navy, and had acquired a tattoo on his forearm.

He usually wore a suit, a wool jacket and trousers with turn-ups, or a three-piece suit, with matching waistcoat and tie.

On special occasions, he favoured his Sports Jacket with cord edgings, with an emblem on the top left front pocket. Upper classes wore bowler hats, while William belonged to the middle classes and wore a trilby hat. Two-tone shoes or brogues were the popular choice of shoe.

Beryl's mother, Annie Elizabeth was born 1902 in Marrickville, Sydney, and was the second of four children Robert, Martha & John, born to Annie Isabell (nee Meale) and John Francis Roden. Her father died when she was nine.

1927 Annie; was an attractive 25 year old woman, who's just a little shorter than her husband, her medium length wavy auburn-hair, highlights her fair skin and pretty pale blue eyes. She has a quiet persona with a good sense of humour and everyone called her 'Topsy.'

A working woman and dress-maker, Topsy liked to dress well and had homemade versions of the fashionable styles. In those days it was a simple shapeless loose-fitting garment that hung from the shoulders with a dropped-waistline.

Her Sunday best outfit usually consisted of either a summer cotton dress with a square neckline, or winter two piece wool or a tweed suit, comprising of sweater and below knee, length skirt.

Hats changed from wide-brim to neat cloches, matched with ankle strapped button shoes.

William and Topsy had been married four years, when after renting places in Ashfield, Kingsland Road in Regents Park in 1923, and Crawford Street, Berala in 1924. they built their own home at 11 Clarke Street, in the quite suburb of Berala, Sydney in 1926. It was funded through William's entitlements of an ex-servicemen's war home loan.

Their two bedroom bungalow styled home, was built with dark bricks and glazed tiles on a broken hip roof. The home has five sturdy brick steps aligned to the Art-deco front door. To the right there's an extended bricked-in porch for outside family living. To the left; beneath the wooden awning covered windows; of the master bedroom Topsy has planted hydrangea shrubs. The big beautiful blue- and pink-blooming clusters of flowers with serrated leaves, was accentuated by the dark brick wall.

The hub of the house was the latter addition of a sunroom connected to the kitchenette, and wooden laundry. The laundry had a washing copper. The sanipan toilet called an outhouse is located down the back-yard.

11 Clarke Street Berala

Front left to right: Topsy, Dot, Nana Roden holding Beryl, Bob, William Wyber, seated in car Uncle Jack Jack.

Original Plans 11 Clarke Street

The Presbyterian Church is the family's place of worship.

An Anniversary Souvenir Booklet (not coloured) is presented to the congregation. The front cover displays the churches Logo of a tree negative, overlayed on a finely striped X-cross. The tree is oval framed with Latin inscriptions ending with a small floral bouquet. At the base another oval ribbon frames the first with the churches name.

> *- Presbyterian Church of Australia-*
> Written below the Logo in Old English Text; it reads-
> *–Lidcombe-Berala   Presbyterian   Church-Anniversary Souvenir-*

A pencil drawn picture illustrates an impressive gable roof brick church, with an expansive stairway leading to colonial glass entrance doors with a Sunrise window above. Chapel windows are on either side. Another five chapel windows runs the length of the church ending with an extensive vestry down the back. The church is located on a V shaped corner block between Crawford and Tilba Street and shielded from the traffic by a double brick fence.

Dated: May 1st, 1927 the insides cover reads –

The Foundation Stones, of the new church had been laid by the Rev W.J. Gray, B.A and Alexander Watt, Esq on December 12th, 1925 and the church completed on 1st May 1926.

On December 11, 1927; William, Topsy, family, and friends gathered together with the congregation to observe, as The Rev G. Nelson Beasley cradles their six week old baby girl in his arms, offering her devotion to God and cleansing from sin.

The Reverend dressed in white blesses her with the Holy water while he utters the words.

"I baptise you...Beryl Winsome Wyber in the name of the father and of the son and the Holy Spirit and of the True Angels."

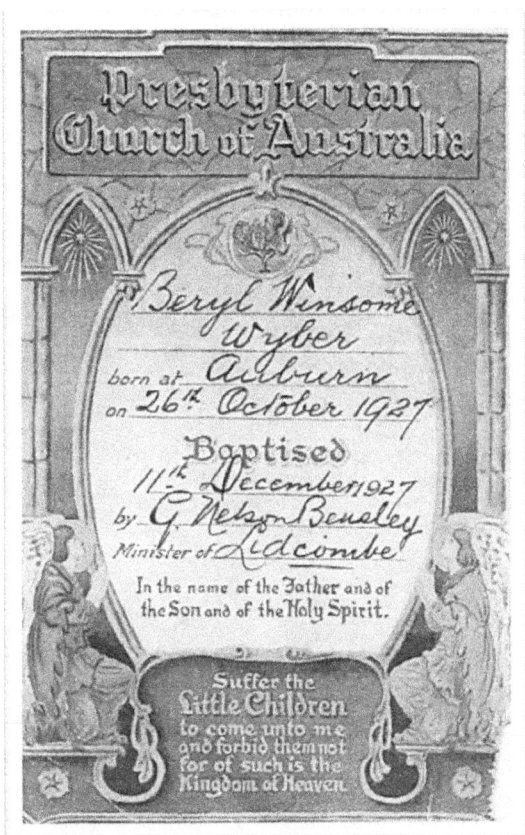

Anniversary Souvenir

The Blue Mountains Holiday

Born a healthy child, her family could not have been prepared for what was about to happen. It was the autumn of 1929, while the family were holidaying with relatives at Katoomba near the Blue Mountains. At some-time and some-how within that holiday the incident occurred.

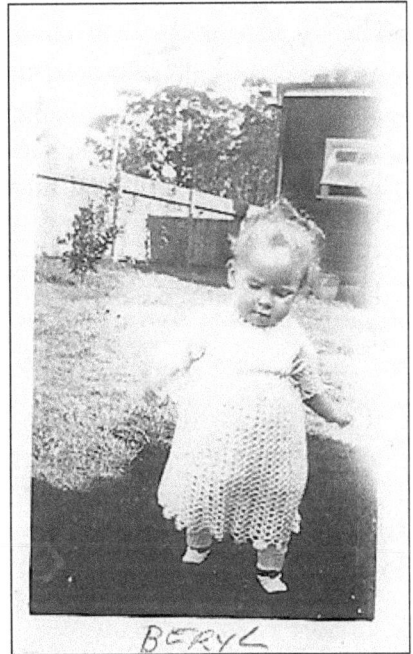

Dot & Beryl Wyber 11 Clark Street Berala

It was alleged that seventeen month old Beryl fell out of her pram. The following weeks she woke in the night crying and coughing with a mild fever. She wouldn't eat and became weak

13

with difficulties walking, then about two weeks after the incident her mother found a lump on her back.

Beryl was taken to the Royal Alexandra Hospital for Children in Camperdown. Arriving at the multi terraced brick building; they entered into a cold and sterile environment, where your rights for individuality and independence were left behind as you comply with the rules. Crossing the large chequered black/white linoleum floor, they stopped at the front desk. She had an appointment to see Dr Robert Wade, a kind-hearted gentleman about 55 years old with a receding white hairline, who wore round rimmed eye glasses.

The Nurse took Beryl from her mother.

An X-ray and blood test (which was a scratch on the inner wrist called a Monteux Test) diagnosed, Musculoskeletal Tuberculosis or TB of the spine, which usually infects another area of the body first before moving into the spine, resulting with varying degrees of weakness and nerve root compression. This potential, deadly infectious disease firstly attacks the lungs and is spread through the air, when an infected person coughs, sneezes, or spits.

It's a most dangerous form because it can cause bone destruction, deformity and paraplegia. In those days there was a Government Scheme to eradicate Tuberculosis, therefore public TB patients were treated free of charge. They said: "The disease was in the early stages and that she could be treated before it became critical."

Distressed! Topsy reluctantly said good-bye to her fair haired little girl. While the dignified and professional Matron Rose Kirkcaldie a small slim woman, assured Topsy that she needn't worry and that "the sooner she left, the sooner her baby would settle down." The hospitals idea was that a complete separation from their parents would help the child make a better adjustment to their illness.

She said: 'Just kiss her goodbye, the quicker the better, we will look after her and in a few months she will be alright to go home.'

The belief of the day was that children don't feel things like adults, they get over things fast.

Tuberculosis was a greatly feared disease.

In 1929 Beryl was one of 228 Tuberculosis cases admitted to the hospital. They took her to the old isolation basement under 'The Faithfull block'' What was happening? [3]

Only a baby, she was afraid of being alone.

She felt so small in the large metal cot that wasn't her bed.
The room so big with the door with a window a long way away, where strangers dressed in white hiding behind masks came to see her. What are they doing with that needle! Scared and bewildered in the loneliness of the night she cries herself to sleep wondering if mummy is ever coming back!

By the end of the year, Beryl was out of the Isolation block and into the main stream of the hospital; where during the course of a year over 10,000 children had been treated...

---

[3] Hand in Hand p130 – p144

Chapter 2

Friday Nov 22, 1929 an early visit from Santa

The children were told Santa Claus is coming! Many of the children were assembled outside the hospital and everyone is anxiously waiting to see Santa. Cripples on crutches, sick children with pale and sunken cheeks along with children wheeled out on stretchers. [4]

Entering the gates of the Royal Alexander Hospital, Santa heralds his arrival with the sound of masses of jiggling bells, attached to hoops on the horse's harnesses. A coachman dressed in top-hat and tails, drives a team of four prancing white stock horses, that's hitched to a white painted carriage, edged with golden scrolls and decorated with images of Christmas bells and holly leaves.

Santa, dressed in his traditional suit, stands and waves to the crowd of cheering onlookers before descending the five wooden steps, which have been hastily set in place by the grounds man. Excited bursts of cheering rise with high pitched cries of delight as the children greet Santa.

---

[4] The Sydney morning Herald 23rd November 1929, page 21

He then swings the sack-full of toys over his shoulder labelled, 'from Santa Claus to the children of the Royal Alexandra Hospital, from his workshop at Anthony Horderns'. Santa's accompanied by two young girls dressed in fairy outfits, their short curly hair decorated with tinsel head bands, and holding star-wands.

After exchanging pleasantries with the establishment, the official photo is taken with hospital officials. The first child to meet Santa and looking a little confused is a two year-old aboriginal boy, dressed in bibbed shorts and short sleeve shirt, his right knee is bandaged.

Santa repeatedly pats his right shoulder while wishing the young boy a Merry Christmas and then points to the cameraman who takes a photo.

Prior to the boy sitting down another group of five boys… then at the last minute a girl, runs to join him Santa quickly assembles the children around him, then everyone smiles while the photo is taken. Santa with a smile and wave of his white handkerchief continues to greet the crowds of children.

Beryl; seated on the ground looks up as he pauses in front of her, bending down he pats her head while greeting her with words of merriment before moving along.

Jolly old Santa then holds hands, pats and kisses cheeks while singing out good-will messages to the gathered crowds of little patients. A little mystified Beryl's eyes followed him until he is out of her sight.

The young girls follow as Santa walks through the hospital grounds and then through the children's wards, were they are too ill to be moved. The large hospital is a gloomy dark place that's cloaked in painful connotations. The metal beds with pull up sides holds little patients clothed in white hospital gowns, sometimes referred to as inmates by the journalist.

Just off the main building on the open veranda, there are more little patients. It's not a sunny veranda, and it can be cold. The veranda has an iron safety fence between brick supports with large pull down blinds to shield them from the weather. The head of each bed is pushed up against the brick wall in a row down the veranda with not much space between them, leaving a narrow walkway.

Each child is fixed into place in some way. Some are strapped on wooden frames; others are in traction some are in pain and some recovering from it. Some are too sick to do anything but be positioned in bed and some happy and shouting in-spite of twisted limbs.

The baby's wards are always filled with helpless small ones; almost impossibly small babies lie wailing with hands in mittens, while others are gasping for breath in the throes of diphtheria. There are burn victims and some who lay patiently positioned in bed all day with broken limbs suspended from swings.

The hospital's full to overflowing some stay in hospital for months and in other cases for years.
Outside more children are located on the rooftop balcony with sun protective winged canopies attached to the top of their beds.

The busy nurses dressed in crisp starched uniforms and cap, rustle whilst they hurry about attending to their little patients. The only way to get a nurse was to call "Nursie, Nursie," but they need to be within earshot to hear. The children had to listen... for footsteps on the polished tiled floor fitting their cries in between the other children who are calling out.

Sister is furious at the disorder-

> "What's all the commotion? Crying is not allowed... it upsets the other children and then the whole ward starts crying and everyone is in trouble, it's nearly as bad as crooked sheets. If you wanted a bedpan, you just have to wait for pan rounds and learn to wee on demand or wet the bed."

The noise is worst after weekly visits.

Hospital's New Kitchen

In 1925 Sister Tanner went to America to study nutrition, when she returned the hospital's kitchen was completely re-modernised. In charge of the new kitchen was Miss Salome Elizenberg an ex-school teacher and trained nurse. The special diet kitchen is where thousands of individual diets were prepared and weighed, they now have new scales, new gas ranges, an enormous new refrigerator, and new sterilizers for the preparation and process for over three thousand baby bottle feedings, each one is different and carefully checked, to reach the infants absolutely germ-free.[5]

---

[5] Hand in hand P154

George Brough

George Brough; as well as everyone's friend, was a carpenter by trade, and a long-time employee of the hospital. He could turn his hand to fix most things around the hospital and did so gladly.

His services ranged from freeing blocked drains, moving beds, carrying children, relocating the piano and catching mice in the nurse's quarters.[6]

The Society for Crippled Children

In 1929 The Rotary Club of Sydney, in an attempt to provide medical care, education and vocational training for children with physical disabilities, firstly needed to identify these children as records were not available.

So a door-knock survey was conducted. Rotarians frequently encountered slammed doors with the stigma of having a disabled child. This resulted in hundreds of crippled children, living out a lonely and obscure life in back rooms of their homes ... children for whom no constructive rehabilitation was then available.

The first Welfare Officer Margaret Watts of the Society wrote that in those days aftercare following hospitalisation was impossible, as there was no-where for children to go. In the public hospitals there were few orthopaedic beds, and there was no organised service for conveying homebound children or those in heavy apparatus, to and from hospital.

_____

[6] Hand in Hand page 104

In 1930 The Society for Crippled Children was registered as a charity. Beryl later benefited from their work.

The Great Depression

In 1929 The Great Depression came along with the crash of the stock market. The Government issued ration books filled with coupons for each person. When a restricted item was bought they handed over a coupon and were only allowed to use a certain number a week.

The poor devils were starving – half a pound of tea and a pound of butter a month. They substituted dripping for butter and meat become scarce.
To survive people planted gardens to produce fruit and vegetables and kept poultry for meat and eggs. In some urban areas co-operatives were formed based on a barter system, to share what was available.

The working class and unemployed, all suffered severe hardship in some form or other.

If parents were unable to find work, children often became the primary income earners, forced to leave school as young as 13 or 14 they were often sacked from their jobs once they reached adulthood to avoid being paid adult wages.

A work for the dole scheme for the unemployed, found occasional relief pay on public works projects, with labouring jobs and the building of roads. But this was barely enough to sustain the workers and their families.

With the worrying effects of the Depression, the family were forced to rent their home in Clarke Street. Heading south to

Wollongong, William a boiler maker by trade, found work as a contractor with BHP Steel Works at Port Kembla. In 1931, off and on, they stayed at 36 Dennison Street in Wollongong here Topsy ran a small boarding house for men working with her husband.

Desperate times require desperate measures.

After losing his job, William's son William Jr. aged 20 (also known as Bill) and his mate Edward Lambert aged 20, took off from the suburb of Auburn in Sydney on a long push-bike ride to Queensland in search of work. With A knapsack strapped on their backs they were heading to Cairns in search of work harvesting the sugar cane.

On April 25th 1932 after travelling approximately 700 miles the two youths browned by the sun arrived in Brisbane. A News Paper reporter from The Brisbane Courier showing some interest in them took their photo, while questioning them about their journey. They show little interest, as they entertain the reporter with short answers to too many questions.

The Photo on page 23 shows: William on the left is much shorter than Edward who's standing beside him.

They are looking away from the camera with a fixed gaze somewhere to the right; their hair is cut in the style of the day short back and sides. Although Edward's thick stock of curls requires the extra help of bees-wax to keep it under control.

A LONG RIDE
25-4-32

These Lads are undertaking a long Cycle Trip in search of work. They have arrived in Brisbane from Sydney, en route to Cairns.

They're dressed in white singlets, dark trousers and their overcoats are folded over the front handlebars.

Edward has additional luggage of a dilly-bag dangling from his handle-bars, his right hand grips the handlebar while the other hand is in his pocket.

William ready to go has both hands on the handle-bars, and his left foot planted on the bike-peddle.

Somewhere along the way they were introduced to what was known as train hopping.

Four months later...
The Brisbane Courier, Thursday 25th Aug 1932, page 20
http://nla.gov.au/nla.news-page1689433

Edward Percival Lambert (20) and William Wyber (20) were charged in the Police court yesterday before Messer's C.J. Bott and T.Foran J's. P., with having travelled between Ipswich and Toowoomba without having first obtaining a ticket.

Senior Sergeant Wilkinson of the railway police said to the men were found hiding in a wagon yesterday morning and admitted having travelled from Ipswich a fine of £1 to include 11/- the amount of the fare in default 48 hours in the cell was imposed.[7]

On returning home to Wollongong, William later found work at the BHP Steel Works as a crane driver.

---

[7] The Brisbane Courier Thursday 25 August 1932, page 20.

Chapter 3

The Sydney Morning Herald, Wednesday August 6th, 1930
Financial *Difficulties 42,220 Patients.*

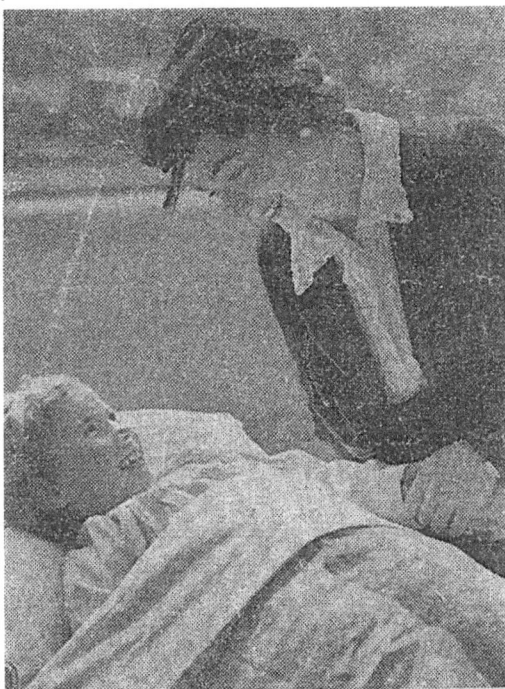

Miss Mollie O'Connor, honorary secretary of the Tall Timbers Ball, talking to
one of the patients at the Royal Alexandra Hospital for Children, yesterday.
The ball will be to-morrow night, and
the proceeds are to go to the hospital.

Beryl Wyber & Miss Mollie O'Connor

The hospital accommodates the ever increasing number of children suffering from the Polio epidemic. Acute cases were transferred to the Royal North Shore Hospital and the Prince Henry Hospital. When the patients reached the convalescent stage - they were taken to the convalescent home at Collaroy.

The Royal Alexandra Hospital for Children stated in the annual report, that the financial difficulties of the board were never greater and that the present situation was viewed with great alarm. By 1931 the hospitals were in such severe financial trouble that the Government proposed a Lottery Bill to support them. The Lottery tickets were priced at five shillings and three-pence and the proceeds were to be paid into consolidated revenue for the 176 hospitals.

Fund Raising

The running of the hospital required vast amounts of money, while the government contributed 30% of the running cost; another 70% had to be found through donations. Despite this, the demands on the hospital and buildings continued to grow. Many people and organizations from all walks of life, rallied to meet the financial needs. Regular annual winter fund raising events Christmas appeals, concerts, bazaars, dances, balls and carnivals just to name a few.

An annual Garden Fete was held on the grounds of the convalescent home at Collaroy, where a total of twelve stalls sold, cakes, produce, kitchenware, jam, fancywork, refreshments and cushions. One special stall was for the sale of articles, toys and other handwork made by the small hospital patients. This is organised by the residents to raise funds for the convalescent home.[8]

The Newspapers served them by publicizing all of the fund raising events ensuring a successful day. It was due to the countless number of people who gave their time to the hospital that it continued to survive.

One man in particular was most notable ...

William Morris - Lord Nuffield (1877 – 1963)

Born in 1877 William Richard Morris later known as Lord Nuffield was one of the first British industrialists to introduce mass production methods.

His Company Morris Motors Ltd, prospered in the years after the First World War. He was a product of the capitalistic system, which enabled him to amass great wealth and he made noble use of it.

He was a philanthropist and over the years he gave generous donations to the Commonwealth in the amounts of £50,000 and £40,000, for care of crippled children.

The main purpose of the money was beds for children suffering from tubercular afflictions of the bones and joints and the treatment in hospitals and convalescent homes.

His generosity was also extended to the education, vocational training and placement in employment. Money was also applied towards modernising hostels and hospitals devoted to treatment

---

[8] The Sydney Morning Herald 2 December 1929, page 5

of crippled children. In addition, he gave other outstanding gifts, for medical research and the treatment of the disease.

Entertainment - The Story Man

Mr W. A. Thompson, a kind hearted school teacher who after returning from the First World War, had decided that after school he would read stories to the children in hospital.

Beryl briefly escaped the hospitals monotony when Mr Thompson made his regular visit, stimulating her imagination reading classic children's stories such as - The Adventures of Huckleberry Finn and Tom Sawyer, by Mark Twain.

His work was so much appreciated, that in 1922 still employed by the Education Department, they relived him of his normal teaching duties to become a full-time official storyteller. From then on he was better known as 'The Story-man,' and was the first of his kind in the world.

Mr Thompson not only engaged the attention of the children by telling them classic stories, he also taught them whatever manual-craft work was possible for their age and condition, in addition to any other form of education that he thought fit.

Singing also played a big part. The children were taught to sing with their teacher and encouraged to do so, while he was away. By this means, many a dull and otherwise profitless hour was passed. His main centre was at the Collaroy branch of the Royal Alexandra Hospital, but it wasn't the only hospital he visited.[9]

On Monday to Friday, at the Trades hall, Mr Thompson also ran a programme on 2KY at 6:30 p.m. called the Children's Hour.

The Hospital Children's Amusement Fund; is a fund having as its object to relieve the boredom of sick and convalescent children during their time in hospital.

It was founded and maintained by the officers and staff of the United Insurance Company.

The regular donations proved sufficient to enable the children to enjoy a few hours enjoyment provided by a Punch and Judy show, concerts by several artists, and also a four valve cabinet set with loud speaker and battery charging apparatus. [10]

1932 Farmers Ltd, Exhibition

From 1:30 p.m. until 3 p.m. all the children worked at handicrafts. They are kept busy preparing for the eighth annual Farmer's Children's Exhibition, where proceeds from the sale of handicrafts were paid to the hospital. The exhibition consisted of nine hundred entries in children's hobbies competition. Conducted by Farmers Ltd and opened at Blaxland Galleries in George Street Sydney for a fortnight.

---

[9] The Sydney Morning Herald Monday 1 May 1922, page 4

[10] Sydney Morning Herald, Tuesday February 9th, 1926, page 6

The competition was divided into 11 classes. The competitors included boys and girls from three to seventeen years of age and school children from every part of the state.

Included were a variety of crafts from:-

- needlework,
- woodwork modelling,
- pottery making
- poetry

A brilliant green cardboard cart with plasticine wheels was the work of the youngest entrant, aged three. A fourteen year old had constructed a miniature loom complete with a navy and white checked scarf in the making, accompanied by complicated instructions.

The small patients produced an amazing quantity and quality of produce. They made knitted wool covered coat hangers, knitted tea cosies, woollen jumpers, baby clothes and the boys could knit as well as the girls. There were embroidered cushions, tapestries, woollen toys and wastepaper baskets.

Boys concentrated on detailed models of aeroplanes and ships, while the girls favoured embroidery designs, some of which showed remarkable neatness.

Routines

The hospital's routine started early in the morning, as the Doctor does his rounds. Beryl was completely institutionalised, due to the day after day year after year domineering and tightly scheduled routines that had been strictly set in place.

She had feelings of helplessness when a lot of things were done at inconvenient times and until she was nine, bed times were at 5p.m. every afternoon.

The controlled environment of the hospital was mundane compared to the world outside, where the excitement of a parade was underway. Saturday 19 March 1932 Beryl was 4 years old. On that day in the midst of the Great Depression, it was the ceremonial opening of The Sydney Harbour Bridge.
Made from 3,200 tons of steel the bridge towers over the suburbs and drew a massive crowd of over 750,000 onlookers.

At the hospital, the nurses listened to the ABC National Radio coverage of the opening... Governor Sir Philip Game opened the official proceedings at 10 a.m. with a congratulatory message from King George V.

The Premier, the Hon J T Lang made a speech and then the announcer described the de Groote incident.

> *"Captain de Groot of the New Guard rode up and slashed the ribbon, exclaiming. 'In the name of the decent and loyal citizens of New South Wales I declare this bridge open..."*

The first to cross the bridge were the politicians and speech makers, followed by a two kilometre long Historic Pageant of twenty seven floats, military bands, war veterans and boy scouts.

Many people had travelled by train to St James station so they could walk across the bridge. At the end of the day the crowds going home had a long wait, finding the line up to the station was jammed because the guards had closed the gates and were only letting a small number through at a time. The Daily Telegraph reported that over 1,000,000 people in trains, trams, vehicles and on foot crossed the newly opened Bridge.

At that time one of the biggest thrills in life was to cross the harbour bridge in an open car and look up at the metal arches.

Nurse holding baby Beryl

Chapter 4

Diphtheria has a nick name... the strangling angel of children.

On Tuesday August 30th 1932, Doctor Wade's name was crossed off Beryl's attendance card, he was replaced by a young out spoken visiting Physician named Doctor Davis.

The Diphtheria Ward

The Sir Charles Percy Barlee Clubbe, Diphtheria Ward was officially opened on Friday February 2nd 1934. The new shoe-box shaped three-story brick building; with a small turret projecting from the centre of the hip roof, was one of the best equipped Diphtheria Ward in Australia. There are two floors containing 63 beds in rooms of various sizes, Nurses, domestic staff and storage occupied two floors.

In 1935 Beryl was in the Diphtheria Ward. Despite the fact that she was extremely ill and finding it hard to breathe, she still managed an endearing smile, when they presented her with a beautiful Doll named Nola.

'NOLA'
Mission fulfilled Beryl's Joy
'Nola', the doll which was annually given from 'The Sun' Newspaper, was a toy funded to the little patient who has suffered longest in hospital and that year went to Beryl Wyber[11]

Hospital Miracle

Lifted from a bed of tissue paper in a big cardboard box by a frail little girl whose hands trembled with eagerness as she struggled up from her pillow.
If you were to look through the big pane of glass, into that ward in the Isolation Block at the children's hospital, you can see a

---

[11] Extract taken from 'The Sun' Newspaper

little girl. She is Beryl Wyber, and she is in the second bed on the right-hand side, you will certainly notice, the big eyes and the fine brown hair that spreads over the pillow.

She is very pale, and very small.

Almost all of her seven years of life, she has spent in the hospital fighting a long battle against the disease which has struck at her spine. Now, into this little girls life has come 'Nola' a lady, to be sure, all dressed in blue, with frills and flounces, and a delicate air. She was made, with infinite care by the 'Two Friends' who present her each year to 'The Sun' Toy Fund.

She entered life yesterday in the hospital ward, when she lit the eyes of little Beryl Wyber with such a light happiness as is seldom seen, and brought a flush to pale cheeks. Nola had fulfilled her mission she had worked a little miracle.

Nola became her constant companion she loved that doll, and was never happier than when she had new clothes for her. Convalescing back at Collaroy she generously allowed her friends Betty, Pat and Shirley to play with Nola too.

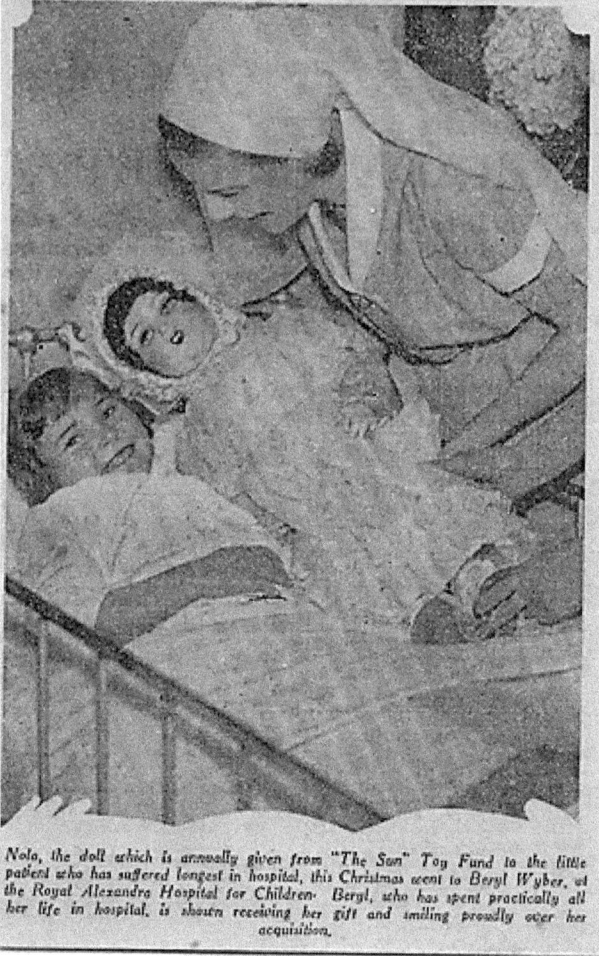

Nola Given To Beryl

Nola, the doll which is annually given from "The Sun" Toy Fund to the little patient who has suffered longest in hospital, this Christmas went to Beryl Wyber, at the Royal Alexandra Hospital for Children. Beryl, who has spent practically all her life in hospital, is shown receiving her gift and smiling proudly over her acquisition.

Nola, the doll which is annually given from "The Sun" Toy Fund to the little patient who has suffered longest in hospital, this Christmas went to Beryl Wyber, at the Royal Alexandra Hospital Beryl, who has spent practically all her life in hospital, is shown receiving her gift and smiling proudly over her acquisition.

36

Contamination

The hospital struggles to keep cross contamination under control not only for patients, but also for the nurses.

Beryl lived with the constant dangers of diseases such as Pneumonia, Scarlet Fever, Measles, and Golden staph.

At The Royal Alexander Hospital at Camperdown the progress of the disease is monitored with a regular X-Ray. They also run tests for typhoid, along with regular throat swabbing for diphtheria. She also suffered skin infections, painful plaster boils called Coetaneous Diphtheria, (a grey-brown membrane related to the continual wearing of a plaster jacket.)

Backwards Camperdown / Forwards Collaroy;

Beryl spent most of her time in the Royal Alexander Hospital for Children at Camperdown; recovery time was spent at the Home in Collaroy.

Chapter 5

The Convalescent Home at Collaroy

The homes original owner and builder was a Mr. George Sargood. In 1921, the home was given to The Royal Alexandra Children's Hospital as a gift by Mr Frederick. G. Sargood.

The Citizen's War Chest Fund gave £5,000 to endow five cots in perpetuity and another £5,000 worth of government bonds, the interest on these to go to upkeep of the convalescent home that had been donated by Mr F. G. Sargood.

The Convalescent home at Collaroy in connection with the main hospital was opened June 24th, 1922 on a Saturday afternoon. In front of a large crowd, the Governor Sir Walter Davidson was accompanied by Dame Margaret Davidson, and received by a guard of honour composed of the Boy Scouts of the Manly and Narrabeen Troops along with the Manly Girl Guides.

The Tudor Revival styled beach house was painted white and enhanced with dark timber, with a red tiled roof. It was situated in Beach Road on prime real estate with magnificent ocean views. Money was also raised to buy land in front of the cottage, to retain for them the beautiful views and for more extensions later on. It had previously been used as a Rest Home for weary soldiers, at the end of the 1st World War.

Mr F.G. Sargood also donated £2,300 to purchase the house next door. A northern veranda was extended this increased the bed capacity from 35 to 60 beds.

A special Solarium was add using Vitaglass to allow the suns healing rays to penetrate and also to protect the children from the cold winds during the winter months, of which Mr F.G Sargood donated £1,000.

Like the hospital; Collaroy relied heavily on Lay staff. These many kind and sympathetic volunteers assisted the trained nurses and helped look after the children. Groups came to read to the children, while young women would teach them fancywork, sewing and bead work.

A generous old lady in Newtown collected comics for them while others gave gifts of clothes, fruit, cakes, toys, and books.

In 1936 Lord Nuffield gave £50,000 to the Commonwealth to help crippled children, of this £2,500 came to the Children's Hospital. The hospital then spent £500 for 5 years for the cost of maintaining the additional 40 beds. Previous improvements included a kitchen fitted with all the latest appliances for cooking, additions to the nurses and maids quarters and a complete boiler installation to provide hot water for the whole of the home.[12]

---

[12]*Hand in Hand page 121*

A large crowd was in attendance as the Federal Minister for Health Mr W. M. Hughes, opened an extension to the original open air pavilion to provide accommodations for another 40 beds, bringing the total to 100 beds. The Nuffield Wing, as it was called, was a veranda about 50ft x 30ft which was built on a slight slant to enable the children to look out over the sea from their cots. The hospital had constructed three wards in front of the house (girls, bubs and boys) which opened onto a wide veranda. The roller doors to the wards were open most of the time and beds were rolled onto the veranda during the day.

On the veranda their beds were placed side by side, to soak up the healing rays of the sun, everyone was brown as berries. Ramps were constructed in front of the pavilion to facilitate the movement of patients in their beds onto the concrete promenade and lawns.

A flower edged path flowed down an extensive grassy slope to a picket fence leading to the beach. Children; Phyllis, Shirley, Laurel, Glennis and Max, who were regular beach goers often visited the convalescent home at Collaroy.

The home being located on the headland, meant when storms from the east-north-east came it delivered blinding rain, and combined with the sound of howling winds, flashing lightning and crashing waves it made every one fearful.

Birthday Cakes

There were some nice moments, and one of those occasions was the rows of iced birthday cakes, which would awaken the acquisitive greedy sense of any child.

After the cakes having firstly played their part; in the 1ˢᵗ Annual Exhibition held by the Master Pastry Cooks Association at the Australian Hall. The cakes were given to the Royal Alexander Hospital for Children for distribution among the young patients.[13]

On 24ᵗʰ December of each year a Christmas tree was assembled in every ward, decorated with different colours streamers, helping to make a happy day for the children. As well as Santa they were visited by the Lady Mayors Mrs George Parks, Dr R B Wade (President), members of the committee, volunteer's helpers, and other workers form the hospital.

Lessons in Bed

Beryl's schooling was not neglected. Schooling was established in May 1922 at the Convalescent Hospital for Children at Collaroy.

Miss Martha Simpson was the originator of the hospital schools in N.S.W. She was one of the states most gifted teachers and an inspector of schools. Teachers were carefully selected and made up of men and women whose gifts include patience, controlled sympathies, and unbounded enthusiasm for their job.

In March 1923 Miss Renouf was appointed to the Basement Ward at the Royal Alexandra Hospital at Camperdown where the patients were mainly long-standing cases of TB, hips, spine, joints etc.[14]

---

[13]The Sydney Morning Herald Wednesday 16 October 1935, page 7

[14] The Sydney Morning Herald, Thursday 14ᵗʰ January 1954, page 4

Education Department Praised

In a letter to the Editor, Marjorie Tanner pays a tribute to the work of the Education Department at the convalescent home at Collaroy of the Royal Alexandra Hospital for Children.

The correspondent states that two teachers and complete equipment keep the little patients occupied from 9am till 3pm Considering their disabilities and lack of early educational facilities, writes the correspondent,

> *"It is wonderful to see the progress the children make. What a blessing it is to think that these children, who are in bed practically the whole of their school life, need not go out into the world backward in learning, as well as in physical fitness."[15]*

Activities

The children liked to play and found various ways to amuse themselves. More able-bodied children would borrow bandages from the physiotherapy room, sharing them with their friends, copying the nurses they would bandage their dolls. They also read books, pieced together jigsaw puzzles that were placed on trays and painted pictures.

---

[15] Sydney Morning Herald Saturday September 15th, 1928, page 22

Beryl also learnt to make silk purses and embroidered doilies, which she would give away as Christmas presents.

This letter to her mother, hints at how she might have felt.

Dear mum,

I am feeling much better today, I was going to write last night but nurse made me put my things away, and I am trying to do my best writing.

When are you going to bring Joan and Dorothy and baby to see me because I haven't seen them for a long time it is the first time I wrote to you for a long time.

So good bye mum

From your loving Beryl Wyber

Xxxxxxxxxxx

Heaven's Special Mum

Beryl & Topsy Wyber
The Royal Alexandra Hospital grounds

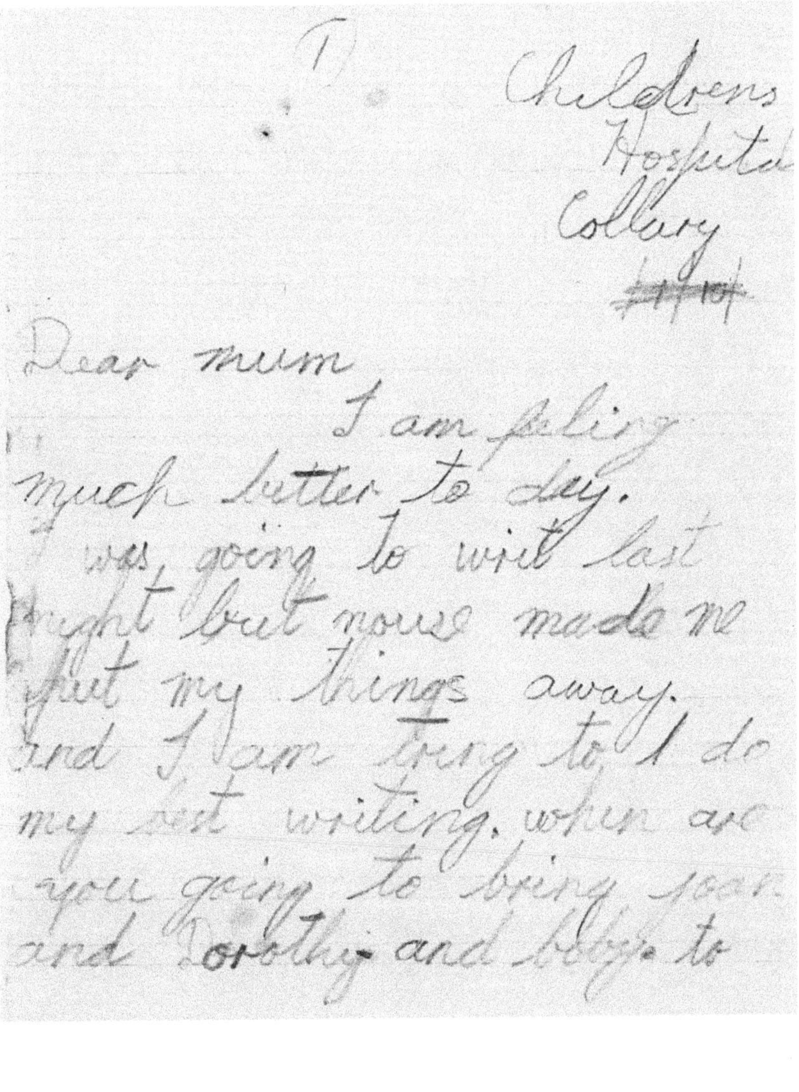

Childrens
Hospital
Collary

Dear mum
        I am feeling
much better to day.
I was going to writ last
night but nouse made me
put my things away.
and I am trying to, I do
my best writing. when are
you going to bring joan
and Dorothy and boys to

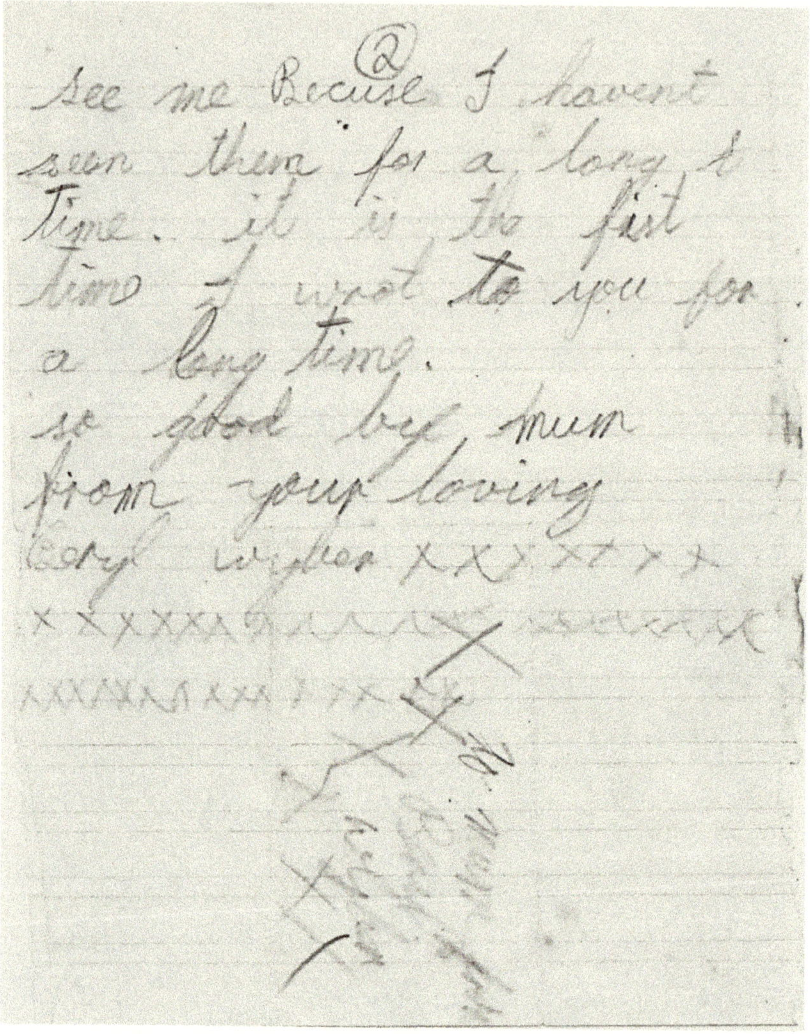

see me Becuse I havent
seen them for a long
time. it is the first
time I wrot to you for
a long time.
so good bye mum
from your loving
[illegible] [illegible] x x x x x x
x x x x x x x x x x x x x x x x
x x x x x x x x x x x x x x

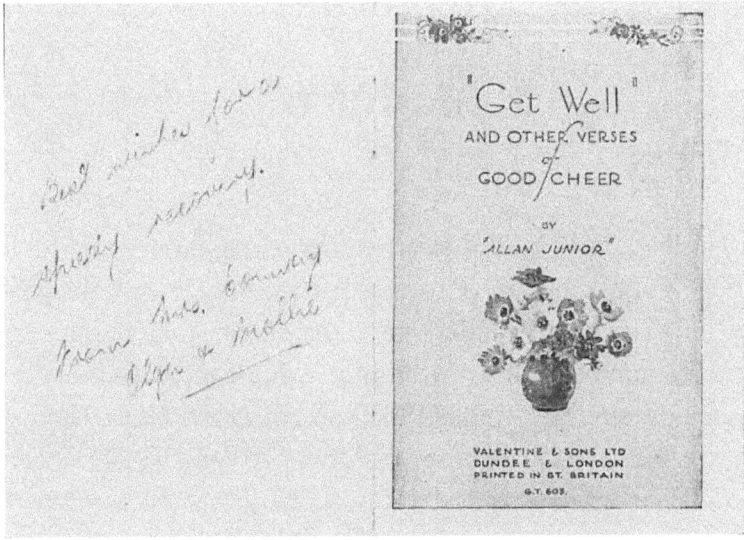

Get well! How very comforting it is,

And how it fills the heart with perfect bliss,

To know that those who care, can thus express

Get Well! —, it's - said sometimes with lovely flowers,

They send to cheer us in our lonely hours-

Gentle reminders, that in Gods domain

Beauty still lives to mitigate life's pain.

47

Chapter 6

6 Staff Street

In 1934 the family moved to a weather board cottage at 6 Staff Street, Wollongong, which was closer to the District Hospital where William was undergoing treatment for Pulmonary Tuberculosis and was later to become a full-time patient. After four years of suffering William died on 20th July, 1936, leaving behind his wife Topsy 34, four children William Jr. 24, Robert 13, Dorothy 11 and Beryl 9.

6 Staff Street Wollongong

On his passing - William senior was aged 14 when he first started working as an Apprentice Boiler-Smith to Thomas-Toward Engineers at St Lawrence Ironworks Newcastle-on-Tyne in England.

Aged 20 he married Elizabeth Bright they had a son and in the family tradition named him William Jr.

Tragically with-in the first year of their marriage, Elizabeth contracted pneumonia and died shortly thereafter.

On 19 Oct 1913 prior to the 1st World War, William was in Australia, where he was known as a Brilliant Sydney football forward.

Returning to England he enlisted in The Royal Navy in the 1st World War. Sunday 9 November 1919, he returned to Sydney aboard the Steam Ship SS. Osterley. He then found work with the Sugar Refining Co in Fiji before returning to Sydney.

In Sydney, William met Annie Elizabeth Roden (Topsy) and were married at the Malvern Hill Methodist Church, Croydon on Saturday 18 November 1922.

William Wyber: Sugar Refining Co in Fiji

Family Deaths Notices

Sydney Morning Herald Monday July 20th, 1936

Wyber July 19th, 1936, at Wollongong District Hospital, William Wyber aged 46 of 6 Staff Street Wollongong, and late of Berala, beloved husband of Annie and father of Bill, Robert, Dorothy and Beryl

---

Funeral Notices

Sydney Morning Herald Monday July 20th, 1936

Wyber- the Relatives and Friends of Mrs William Wyber and Family of 6 Staff Street, Wollongong, are invited to attend the Funeral of the late beloved Husband and their father to leave Wollongong District Hospital this (MONDAY) afternoon at 1'Oclock for Woronora Crematorium Service at 2:15 pm

H. Parsons, Funeral Director Wollongong.

Return Thanks Notices

Sydney Morning Herald

August 15th, 1936

Mrs Wyber and Family sincerely thank all relatives and friends for expressions of Sympathy, Letters, Cards, and Floral Tributes in their recent bereavement also Sisters and Nurses of Wollongong Hospital for their kind attention.

Chapter 7

Hospital Visiting Hours Sunday 2pm - 4pm

Topsy quite enjoyed the Sunday visits to see Beryl. While travelling back and forth on the old steam train from Wollongong to Sydney, it gave her a chance to sit down and relax while enjoying the ever changing scenery. She found companionship with other travellers, with conversations leading to problems they faced. They shared pictures of their families, and over time many strong friendships were formed.

To go to Collaroy from Wollongong the trip firstly by train could take up to two hours before arriving at Central Station. Then a short electric train ride to Circular Quay before a short walk to the green/cream Manly Ferry for a 40 minute trip to Manly. This was mostly pleasurable, although sometimes heavy swells created rough weather making the trip unpleasant.

Over the years Topsy found the harbour views quite interesting, witnessing the construction of the Sydney Harbour Bridge. The newspapers of the day reported the bearings for the bridge, weighing 290 tons each and on each of them the bridge thrust its entire weight of nearly 22,000 tons.

The final connection was to catch the green/cream electric Tram displaying the two-digit route number. The journey from Manly through Queenscliff, North Manly, Brookvale and Dee Why, took about 40 minutes before arriving at Collaroy for the two hour visit. In comparison a trip to the Royal Alexandra Hospital from Central by Tram was a 15 to 20 minute journey.

Topsy Wyber and Nanna Roden

Meanwhile at the hospital, the young nurses were busy trying to get through their work. They spend the morning getting the children ready, putting bows in their hair and making them look nice for the weekly visits.

Topsy would stop off at the old canteen located just past the main foyer to buy Beryl a bottle of 'Marchant Lemonade' and Ice-Cream-Sundae which was served in a glass dish.

Propped up in bed with pillow support Beryl's short cropped wavy hair was tied with a band of ribbon around her head.

Seeing her mother she instantly lights up with a welcoming smile. Embracing one another with hugs and kisses, Topsy then slides the Sunday Comics from the Newspaper over to her eager hands.

She tells her mother any news, both good and bad, over the years she'd witnessed many sad events. Then settles down to devour her ice cream while listening attentively to the news of what's been happening within the family. She felt a part of the family but at the same time felt apart from it.

Despite all the problems, her mother was always there to provide her with the all-important support, encouragement and confidence she needed to keep going. Topsy had faith that one day their prayers will be answered and with God's help, Beryl would get better so she could come home.

At the end of the ward high up on the wall, housed in an ornate wooden-case, there's the homely symbol of a large round faced grandfather clock. The sound of the arrow pointed hands, solemnly tick-*Tock* tick-*Tock* around the clock, while the mesmerizing pendulum swings to and fro, the precious minutes and hours quickly disappear. Then beginning with a little tune the grandfather clock chimes four times.

Topsy looks up then turning to Beryl says: "It's time to go" a prolonged embrace of her mother hints that Beryl's fretful feelings have return once more, but long ago she'd learnt not to cry.

Doctors' Orders

The hospital is extremely strict, especially with bed rest. Doctor's orders:

> "Whilst there is a rise of temperature the patient should be kept at rest in bed. If this fails to effect improvement, absolute rest may be necessary".

When on absolute rest, the patient has to lie in bed. Doctors' orders states that:

> "Beryl is not allowed to do anything for herself, being washed and fed by nurses, and may not read, knit, or sew and not write letters".

If any visitors were allowed it must only be for a few minutes at a time as she must not suffer any fatigue. Polished dark brown leather straps with large buckles, lined with a thick felt were secured around the waist and hips, while the legs were pinned in a V shape. Once locked in place a white hospital sheet displaying a red cross, covered the hoop. Beryl would undo those straps not to be naughty, but because she was fearful that if she didn't exercise the muscles, they'd become useless.

While lying in bed, she thought about walking and started moving her legs going through the motions and pretending to walk. The punishment for disobeying doctor's orders was to be put in the babies ward and many times that's where she would end up. In the bub's ward, some of the children have congenital dislocation of the hips and they are called 'Froggies.' Their hips and legs are set in a plaster cast with their knees bent at right angles to their waist and they have to lie on their tummy sometimes for up to 18 months.

The hospitals well-used beds showed their age. The mattresses stuffed with coconut fibre and placed on a board were extremely hard and uncomfortable, but Beryl had gotten use to that over the years. Although life wasn't great Beryl always had a ready smile and found contentment and happiness living in the moment of each day, alongside of her hospital friends Coral, Alice, Bob, Noel, Martin, Shirley, Betty, Pat, and Clines. She was never alone.

Betty, Beryl & Pat at Collaroy

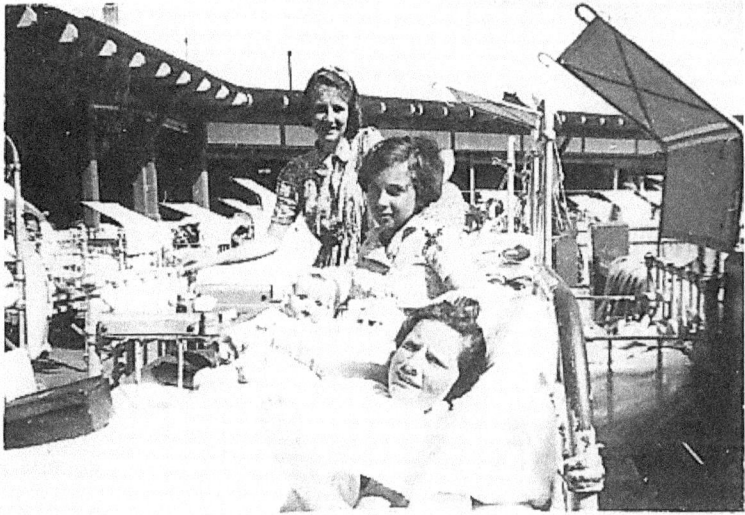

The Reverend Dobbinson - visited the convalescent children in Collaroy, and regularly made visits at the St Giles home in Tasmania (which he helped establish). His passionate support for children with disabilities, especially those affected by polio, was probably one of the motivations for making this 1:40 length film in 1940 in which Beryl was seen between 1: 15 to 1: 22   the scenes of children in the forty minutes of colour footage are incredibly vivid. The treatment methods, rehabilitation facilities and arcane harnesses the children are made to wear are those of a bygone era. For this reason the film is an important document of how children affected by polio and other crippling diseases were treated in the 1940s.

Chapter 8

William Morris - Lord Nuffield (1877 – 1963)

Cheers for Lord Nuffield, as the children welcome his visit. The small patients at the Crippled Children's Convalescent Home of the Royal Alexandra Hospital for Children at Collaroy gave an enthusiastic welcome to Lord Nuffield when he visited them yesterday afternoon.

Lord Nuffield arrived and walked up the ramp to the veranda of the hospital, as the children cheered and sang, "For He's a Jolly Good Fellow".

Now ten years old Beryl had more knowledge of the man who supported people like herself. Enjoying the fun and excitement of the day Beryl wholeheartedly sang and cheered the man who played an important role in her life.

His tour of the hospital was conducted by Matron Esplin. He stopped at a bed in the first ward, where Dulcie, a nine-year-old patient was treasuring a small parcel. "Lord Nuffield" she said: "will you please accept this gift from the children in this ward". In the parcel were covers for golf clubs, knitted by the children. Eric, who has spent five of his eight years in hospital, gave Lord Nuffield a calendar map of Australia, done in fretwork (a decorative design that is carved on a solid background) by the children.

Billy, a boy of thirteen years, who had been in hospital for ten years, gave Lord Nuffield on behalf of the children in the Nuffield wing, a folding waste-paper basket.

"It has been a very pleasant visit', Lord Nuffield said as he was leaving, 'and I am highly satisfied with the work that is being done in this home. For its size it is at least equal to the best of its kind in the world".

"In cases like these, you have to start with the children, and not wait until they are eighty years of age", He said "The children are treated here, and instead of spending their lives in bath-chairs, they will become healthy citizens. Directly a child is found to be suffering, some action should be taken.

The trouble in Australia is that many children are born in the outback far away from doctors. For that reason there are more crippled children in proportion in Australia and New Zealand than there are in England. Voluntary methods are better than official methods for directly an institution becomes official; it begins to work too much like a machine."

As he left, Lord Nuffield blew kisses to the children, and waved his hand. Lord Nuffield was so pleased with the use of the money he had previously donated that he gave a further £5,000 to the Convalescent home and another £5,000 to the main hospital.[16]

Crippled Children Cheer Lord Nuffield Sydney. Tuesday –

"The patients in the crippled children's convalescent home of the Royal Alexandra Hospital for Children at Collaroy gave an enthusiastic welcome to Lord Nuffield when he visited them this afternoon.

Lord Nuffield is the guest of the Governor General (Lord Gowrie) at Admiralty House.

He will remain there until Thursday, when he will leave for Canberra where he will be the guest of the Prime Minister (Mr Lyons)."[17]

[16] The Sydney Morning Herald Wednesday February 17th, 1937, page 16

[17] *The Argus - Wednesday Feb 17th, 1937, page 8*

Chapter 9

Life without William

The Sydney Morning Herald
Saturday July 17th, 1937 p15
Wyber - In Loving memory of my dear husband and father, son-in-law; William who passed away July 19, 1936; Inserted by his loving wife, children and mother-in-law, A. Roden Lidcombe.

———————

Life without William was a lonely and hard one, for Topsy. Being a lone parent, the demands and burden fell heavily on her shoulders. In those days, there was no support from the government so she worked scrubbing floors, and making dresses to find the money to make ends meet. With the heavy work load she had to carry, there were times when she was unable to make the trip to see Beryl because her own health suffered. As she aged the knuckles on her hands began to show the painful signs of Rheumatoid arthritis and her hair went snow white.

Sometimes you would hear her say: "With the luck I'm having, I think I must have killed a Chinaman."

Almost twelve now, Beryl had lived for the moment. The many photos of her always confirmed a happy child, with a ready smile and joyful eyes, except for one photo. It's a sunny day out on the veranda at the Collaroy hospital; she's propped up with pillows. Her mother call's her name; she looks up from reading the comics, as the photo is taken. In this photo, there was no smile, instead in her eyes there's a look of depression, overhung with a worrying frown and a look of discontent.

Perhaps she had stopped living in the present and was now looking at a bleak-future. Contemplating an eternity, bedridden in hospital and that was a fear-provoking thought.

Topsy now 37, had been widowed for almost three years. Maybe she was sensing Beryl needed her more now, because she decided to move from Wollongong back to 11 Clarke Street to be closer to the hospital.

Encouraged by her mother, they both prayed every night for a miracle. However they also knew that God helped those who helped themselves and it would take an incredible sense of will-power, for this miracle to happen.

When the lights went out, careful not to be heard, Beryl plants her feet on the floor then tries to walk. At times, negative thoughts of hopelessness, followed by tears, fears and frustration overwhelm her when it wasn't progressing as fast as she wanted it to.

Around that time, Beryl wasn't the only one fighting for their freedom.

The World had been plunged into the Second World War.

News Flash - World War II

September 1st, 1939 without warning Germany invaded Poland starting World War II. By the evening of September 3rd, Britain

France was at war with Germany and within a week, Australia, New Zealand, Canada and South Africa had also joined the war.

Her brother, Bob Wyber had now completed his studies at Wollongong High School.

> Sydney Morning Herald Thursday 11th Jan, 1940
> Leaving Certificate Examination Results:
> First A- Class Pass, Second B - Class Pass.
> Wyber, Robert: 1B English, 3B French, 5A Mathematics I,
> 6A, 6B, Mathematics II, 10A Physics, 11A Chemistry.

On 1st Oct 1940, with the event of the Second Word War, Bob enlisted with the Royal Navy Reserve as an ordinary seaman serving in the Navy. He started with the Department of supply then later went on to become an Officer in the Royal Australian Navy.

Girl guides: The Extension Branch

It was around this time Beryl was approached and enrolled with The Post-Guides Extension branch. This brings a new interest into her life – helping her, to develop her own abilities by doing something active for others, and keep her in touch socially. Above all, the Guides will teach her the widest and deepest interpretation of the law of courage and cheerfulness.

The extension branch of the association had grown that year, with recruits being received from the ranks of those children affected by infantile paralysis.

The 10th Post Guides; in which were enrolled all Guides who still had physical disability this branch takes into the movement disabled and invalid girls at home and in hospital or are institutionalized and recruit children affected by infantile paralysis.[18]

Pen Pals

http://nla.gov.au/nla.news-article17672219

Extracted from the Sydney morning herald……..

In Response to;

A recent appeal for letters;

From readers;

On behalf of a group of children in the convalescent home,

Mrs Shaw, of Wagga, was doing good work with a correspondence scheme, chiefly among members of the district rural school.

The school children write to children in hospital, who would appreciate receiving letters of cheer from our readers, and their parents provide a small subscription to help with postage. Names were given in short lists a few at a time.

Here are some patients at the Royal Alexander Hospital, Collaroy who will welcome letters: Bruce Cotterill, Allan Nott,Ronald Bartlett, Kathleen Sealey, Shirley Cryer, Valerie Buckle, Beryl Wyber, Bernie Butler, Keith Wane, and Thelma Porter.[19]

---

[18] *The Argus Saturday 25 November 1939 page 17*

[19] Jan 18th, 1940 the Sydney Morning Herald

Christmas & New Year Greetings

THIS TELEGRAM HAS BEEN RECEIVED SUBJECT TO THE POST AND TELEGRAM ACT AND REGULATIONS

OFFICE OF ORIGIN	WORDS	TIME LODGED	NO.	T.G.42C.
SYDNEY SUB	15	12 32 PM		

MRS WYBER
CAMBRIDGE STREET
LIDCOMBE

CONGRATULATIONS ON BERYL'S RECOVERY HAPPY AND PROSPEROUS NEW YEAR

HENA

R9 - 1 15 PM

Chapter 10

Lucky 13

Beryl was 13 years old, when The Superintendent Dr Ratcliff said that she could go home - in a few weeks. Beryl was so excited that he said: "she could go home as soon as her mother called for her."

Camperdown Chronicle & Geraldton Guardian & Express

The case of Beryl Wyber, 13 years, now discharged from the Children's Hospital, Sydney, after being an inmate since she was seventeen months old, was described as miraculous. The girl suffered from the effects of a spinal injury, but was cured by massage and treatment.

The hospital authorities believe that Bruce Cotterell, 12 years, who has been bedridden since he was an infant, will be able to walk soon. [20], [21]

---

[20] Camperdown Chronicle: Tuesday 7th Jan 1941

[21] Geraldton Guardian and Express Tuesday 21 January 1941 p 1

Potts Point
Jan 1ˢᵗ, 1941

Dear Mrs Wyber.

I felt such a great joy when I heard over the wireless today of the wonderful cure effected on a child with spinal trouble, and that she had been in hospital since she was 17 months old. Although no name was mentioned I immediately called out Beryl Wyber.

And my friend, with whom I board said yes, heard that is the name. I saw it in the paper and meant to tell you. Barry and I were down at Collaroy about 2 months, ago and matron told us there was every prospect of Beryl being discharged.

Although I spoke to Beryl she did not remember me, which was not to be wondered at because the last time I saw her she was in the Diphtheria Ward at Camperdown, when Barry had his last operation and Barry has been home 7 years.

Oh Mrs Wyber what a wonderful New Year's Gift God has given you, I suppose you often despaired of Beryl ever recovering. Usually I am feeling like the young girl. I am absolutely thrilled at her recovery. By your picture you have matured somewhat since the days when we travelled on the Manly Ferry of course I must not mention the age that has crept up on me.

What a relief for you, I know that you're going backwards and forwards to the hospital are over. I used to think Barry would never get well, but when I think you have nearly thirteen years of it, since as long as I had with Barry. What a tremendous joy it must be for you, and as I share a little of your sorrow I wanted to show you the joy I felt at Beryl's recovery.

Well dear I will close again expressing my joy at Beryl's recovery.

And remain

Yours Sincerely.... Mrs Parks

St John's Road
Glebe
1/1/41

Dear Beryl,

I was reading about you in the paper the other day and I was very pleased to hear you are home with your people after so long in hospital. I am a member of Uncle Toms young 2SM and I would like to send you a, cheerio call to you every Monday if you should listen in, I sing between five and six o'clock.

I would so much like you to be my penfriend. I am 11 years old. Would you please answer this letter?

Your Sincere Friend
E. Black

A letter from a nurse
Scottish Hospital
Cooper Street
Paddington

My Dear Baby Lamb,

First and foremost darling congratulations on your wonderful achievement, what a surprise for me to pick up the paper and see your cheeky grin beaming out at me!

Do you remember me coming in to see you on Xmas Eve! I talked to you and the nurse but you very soon snoozed off to sleep again; Many thanks for your Xmas card and present honey, I shall always keep them as a reminder of the bravest little girl I ever knew!

68

I'll just bet this has been the happiest Xmas & New Year of your life well all I can wish you is lots more of them and best of luck always ; drop me a line whenever you can chick.

Until I hear from you, remember sometimes
You're Pal always.... Betty T   xxxxx

The Sunday Telegraph
http://nla.gov.au/nla.news-article55762765
4th January 1941
Her words... recorded in the papers of the day...

> "I wanted mummy to come straight away, and I nearly cried when they said she wouldn't be able to come until tomorrow. I have a brother of 17 and a sister of 15 and they have told me all about my home, but I just can't wait to see it''.

The hospital advised her, that maybe in a month or so she could start trying to walk. The doctors were quite surprised, when on that day she just got up and walked out. Her mother said:

> "I thought we never get away from the hospital gates, as Beryl was so intent on watching where all the people were going."

They finally left the hospital driven home by a taxi. She was very quiet in the taxi. This is the first time she has seen the world, and there was so much for her to look at. When they reached the house, she didn't want to get out of the taxi.

Home at last

The newspaper reporters were there to capture that moment. When her mother and her aunt; helped Beryl out of the taxi. She stood still holding their hands, gazing around at other houses, and the cousins and friends who had come to greet her. Small for her age, Beryl has a bright, attractive face with a radiant smile. Her voice was surprisingly strong, and she laughs with a deep, infectious chuckle. She was rather breathless about this, the biggest day in her life.

Topsy & Beryl Wyber posing for photographers

70

She wore the first real frock she has ever owned, a red-and-blue dirndl with white openwork socks and red leather slippers.

"We bought her new cloths this morning" said her Aunt Margaret, Mrs Jack.

Her aunt said;

> 'She didn't like her new dress much. She wanted something much more fanciful, but she is going to choose some new clothes for herself.'

Beryl posed like a veteran for the photographers, then went up the stairs to the front door with a tense, expectant look on her face.

Her grandmother helped her into the sitting room, and she bounced delightedly on to the well sprung sofa.

Beryl, accustomed to lofty, white walled hospital wards, looked across to the velvet window hangings and said, "Oh, isn't it dark in here!" "Whatever are those?" she asked her mother, pointing to two wooden pot-plant stands. She was suddenly quiet and seemed a little ill at ease among the pictures and cushions, until her mother unpacked her dolls and put them in her arms. She was much more interested in the parcel of hand knitted dolls clothes given to her by the sisters at the hospital than in her own clothes.

The news reporter asked what she wanted to do and see first when she was settled at home. She said; "Oh, I don't know," she said breathlessly,

> 'But I'll probably be going to school with other children. We had school at Collaroy. I liked spelling best; I was good at that."

Then she confided in a near whisper, "But I hate sums."

Beryl has informed her family that she is going to call on all, the neighbour's. Beryl then went on a tour of the house, first of all visiting the bedroom she will share with her sister Dorothy.

Beryl fingered the white bed covers on the two beds, and the crystal dressing table things and chuckled at her own refection in the mirror.

Then she rubbed her slipper along the carpet to feel its texture. She had expected, she told the family, that her bedroom would have a tiled floor like the hospital. In the breakfast-room and kitchen there were frequent pauses while a mystified Beryl was told what the stove, the kitchen cabinet, and the safe were for.

Then she was introduced to Micky the family dog, barking frantically in the backyard and to Puss and her two tiny black kittens. Beryl grabbed the two kittens and wanted to know, "Have you christened them yet?"

They returned to the front room and Beryl was once more enthroned on the sofa, surrounded by her dolls. "Do you like the home?" her Aunt asked.

"Oh it's lovely," she said, looking up at her mother. Beryl's pretty mother Topsy seemed even more excited than her daughter. "It's wonderful to have her home at last," she said. [22]

---

[22] The Australian Women's Weekly January 11, 1941. Page 15,

Beryl said:

"She'd expected to be able to walk when the doctors said she could try. I use to slide out of my bed every night for a week before I went home.

In bed, I'd pretend I was walking – just lifting my feet off the floor, they felt so strong, I knew, I'd walk when I got up."

She said: -

"It's so wonderful to see people walking about and the trams and cars, and the new houses and shops. Now I've seen mummy's house all I want to do is walk around inside all day.

It's so different from the hospital. Later I want to see a movie; Barbara Stanwyck and Robert Taylor are my favourites.

I've read all about them, I want to go to the Zoo, in the boat, ride on an electric train, and go to the beach."

Nancy McNally, Beryl Wyber, Margaret Hopkins

Extracted from the Sunday Telegraph

Front cover top *left reads*: http://nla.gov.au/nla.news-page4713934

Sydney Child sees the World for First Time

The front cover picture of the magazine overshadows her story, with a full page coloured photo of a War Ship an A.I.F Contingent, leaving for overseas service, along with news concerning Troops in the War.

On her return home, The Sunday Telegraph took Beryl 'Just around the corner' where she thought everything was – taking pictures of her at the sea, the city, the Zoo, Luna Park and her playing with two other children with kittens.

In hospital Beryl's teachers and her mother had told her about the outside world and had shown her pictures of many things, but there were many things no one thought to tell her about - simple things to know, things that most of us take for granted. Carpets at first intrigued her she would lift them up to see what was underneath.

"What is that?" asked Beryl, pointing to an electric fan. On

74

being told, she raised an exploring hand. Drawers fascinated Beryl, who spends a lot of her time at home in Berala pulling them out and investigating their contents.

The Harbour Bridge was so un-expectantly big. Sydney's size too surprised her. Beryl builds her first sand castle (at Balmoral Beach) "It tickles" she said, as she walked her barefoot on the sand, and went for her first paddle in the water. In the hospital Beryl often dreamed of playing on the beaches.

At Luna Park, On Nero's back, Beryl discovers the delights of the merry-go-round. It was her first ride. She visited Noah's Ark (she laughed happily when she saw herself in the distorting mirrors.
Beryl makes friends with a koala, at Taronga Park. Her first wish was to see a koala, "she expected him to be smaller."[23]

---

[23] *The Sunday Telegraph Pictorial January 12th, 1941*

A Poem especially written for Beryl was among the 50 letters, telegrams, and cards received since her release from hospital, the letters were from all parts of N S W.

The Poem,

A Ray of Sunshine
I saw a picture of you Beryl
You looked so happy at heart
You were hand in hand with Mother
Walking along your garden path
What a ray of Sunshine,
This has brought into your home,
To see a little girl return
able to walk alone.
For twelve long years you lay
in the Children's Ward,
Now God has given you strength
To walk of your own accord
Your dear Mother perhaps thought
This would be impossible
Praise to the Doctors and Nurses
Of the Royal Alexander Hospital"

Girl receives gifts, poem

A poem especially written for her was among the 50 letters, telegrams, and cards received by Beryl Wyber, 13, of Berala, since her release from hospital.

She was admitted to the Royal Alexandra Hospital for Children when she was 10 months old, suffering from a spinal injury.

Beryl walked for the first time four days before she went home on December 30 last.

The poem, written by "A Well-Wisher," Summer Hill, was called "A Ray of Sunshine."

The letters from all parts of New South Wales included one from a five-year-old boy at Northbridge.

Beryl has also received 19 presents, 13/6 in postal notes, and boxes of flowers.

This "fan-mail" was sent after the Sunday Telegraph Color-Pictorial published last Sunday a series of photographs of Beryl.

The Sunday Telegraph took Beryl to the beach, the city, the zoo, and to Luna Park and showed in pictures her reactions to all these new experiences.

By M. M. English 30th Dec 1940

Chapter 11

1941 Exciting New World

With all the excitement; of a Hero's welcome home now starting to fade. The realization that although this was her family, Beryl knew very little of the families routines. Standing on her own two feet came with new rules and responsibilities and up until now, there had been very little to do in looking after herself. At times she missed the Nursing Sisters and friends who were like family to her.

Not long out of hospital, there was sadness, when Beryl's Uncle Robert Roden, aged 41, died.

He was Topsy's eldest brother.

The Sydney Morning Herald Thursday 8 January 1942 page 14

RODEN.-In memory of my dear son and Brother, Robert, who passed away 8 January, 1941 - Inserted by: his mother and sisters.

Berala School

It was time to face the challenges of fitting into society and her first challenge was going to a normal school. Berala School was located within a short walking distance from her home.

She was starting here in 5th Class; with forty other healthy robust children. Even though the teachers keep an eye on her, along with rules and regulations to follow, and she was not allowed to join in vigorous physical actives Beryl challenged herself to keep-up. Until the doctors words had to be listened too, both Beryl and Topsy had been warned by the doctor that most children had a relapse in their teenage years because they tried to do too much, got overtired and ended up back in hospital.

The Class of 1941 Berala
Front row 7th from left Beryl Wyber

School 1942

Meningitis

Only a year out of hospital Beryl was having problems, high temperatures, severe headaches, stiff neck, confusion, vomiting and was unable to tolerate light or loud noises. She was distressed to find herself back in hospital.

A needle, inserted into her spinal canal, extract a sample of spinal fluid. The result was meningitis; this was classified as a Medical Emergency. The inflammation's proximity to the brain and spinal cord can lead to serious long-term consequence of deafness, and epilepsy. The usual treatment for meningitis was a week in hospital dosed up on Sulphonamide drugs.

The following year Beryl was in 6th class along with thirty-seven other girls, it was her final year.

Topsy, Dot, Beryl Wyber & Dot Waller

Subs in Sydney Harbour 1942

The War was more evident when it came closer to home. In the early morning hours of June 1, 1942, three Japanese midget submarines snuck into Sydney Harbour, and launched an attack on The U.S Navy Cruiser Chicago, stationed at the Garden Island Navy Base.

One of the local kids named Skeeter and his mates, saved up their pennies so they could catch the Manly Ferry across the Harbour. They hung over the side of the Ferry, while their eyes scanned the sea to spot the periscope of the Sub; they planned to tie a bag over the periscope if they saw it.

Okey Fitton ran the general store. He was also a volunteer Air Raid Warden for the National Emergency Services.

Okey; recruited the local kids that had push-bikes, to carry messages in case of air raids; and Skeeter was one of them. However secretly Skeeter hoped his courage wasn't tested, because they probably would have found him hiding underneath the bed shielding his mum.

The Army closed the beaches, when they had target practice. No-one was allowed on them. Undeterred, Skeeter and his mates crawled through the zigzag course of barbwire, so they could surf.

December 1942

Topsy was the glue that held them all together, the matriarch of the family. She had worked long and hard for the family and had been widowed now for nearly six and a half years. In middle age she was still a fine looking woman well-dressed and groomed. Some time ago, while travelling back and forth on the trains she had met a tall lean man with dark wavy hair named John Burkhardt.

John; in his early 40's was a stylish dresser who mostly wore a three piece suit white shirt and dress tie, habitually smoked a pipe.

Before John came to Australia in 1925 he lived with his family in a small farming community in Alten, Switzerland, located not far from the German border. Although he spoke English well, he still had a slight accent. Topsy, now free of all debts and after a long courtship, accepted John's proposal.

They were married on the 19th December 1942 at the Wesley Chapel Sydney.

Brother's Engagement

Her brother; Bob Wyber had known Nancye Vaughan, better known as (Nan) since their early school days in Wollongong.

When Nan had completed her schooling, her parents enrolled her in Finishing School.

Her education at finishing school was learning the dos and don'ts in society with the idea of bringing assurance and poise.

That comes from not only knowing what to do, but also knowing what not to do.

When Bob returned home from duties in the War, they met up again and he asked her to marry him. Announcing their engagement in the paper, they were married in 1946 at Wollongong.

The Sydney Morning Herald

Saturday December 9th, 1944. Page 24

Family Notices Engagement-

Wyber – Vaughan the Engagement is announced of Nancye, only daughter of Mr. Mrs. Raymond Vaughan, of Wollongong to Robert (Sub- Lieut., R.A.N.V.R) son of the late W. Wyber of Wollongong and Mrs J Burkhardt of Berala.

Sister's wedding

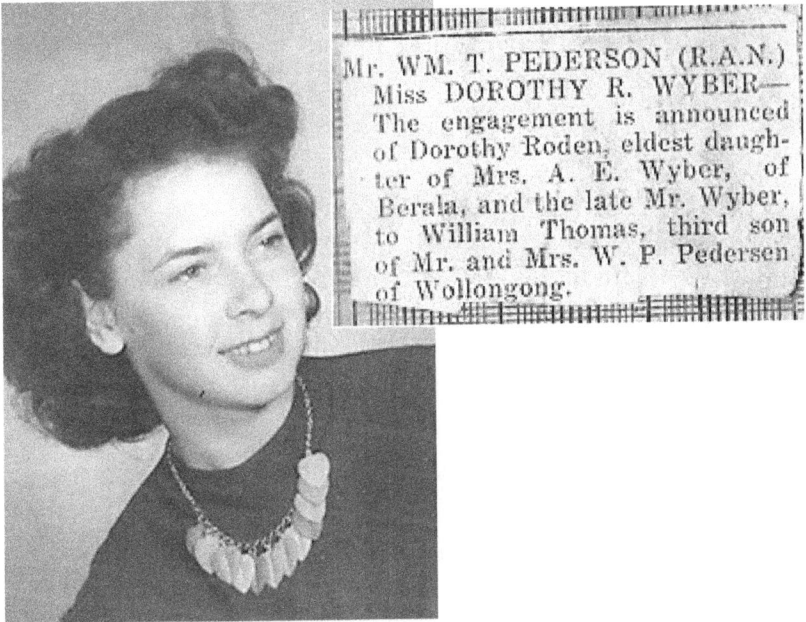

Mr. WM. T. PEDERSON (R.A.N.)
Miss DOROTHY R. WYBER—
The engagement is announced
of Dorothy Roden, eldest daughter of Mrs. A. E. Wyber, of
Berala, and the late Mr. Wyber,
to William Thomas, third son
of Mr. and Mrs. W. P. Pedersen
of Wollongong.

Dorothy Wyber

Dorothy was called Dot by family and friends, a more admirable person would be hard to find. In her early years, she loved to dance and had taken part in several presentations, as a pupil of Miss Zewknoff, who was a well-known dancing teacher in Wollongong.

On Dec 16th 1944, Dot was 19 years old and marrying her childhood sweetheart twenty year old William Thomas Pedersen, a good looking man some people called him Bill or Pedro. Dot lovingly called him Pete, he affectionately called her Kitty.

With an air of command and a love of the Irish, he was a junior Officer in the Australian Navy.

His parents William and Mary Pedersen, having moved from Lithgow came to Wollongong looking for work at the Steelworks. William had attended Wollongong High School, where he first meet and became friends with her brother Bob. The two families become good friends, around the time Dot's father William died, Dot was eleven then.

Dot looked radiant on her wedding day with a smile to match. Her brilliant white satin bridal gown was hand made by her mother, after saving many coupons to buy the material. Her short Brunette hair was crowned with a long flowing wedding veil, and bridal headpiece.

She held a cascading bridal bouquet of assorted flowers. John Burkhardt escorted her down the aisle in the family's Presbyterian Church at Lidcombe-Berala.

Waiting at the altar, William looked self-assured and fine. He was dressed in his Naval Officers Uniform, a blue/black double-breasted woollen tunic, with eight distinctive brass buttons; on his cuffs were gold-braid insignia to indicate his rank. In the crook of his arm, he held a black/white visor cap, with the emblem of the Crown of England, (a silver anchor displayed between golden leaf sprays).

A black & white photo, taken just after the ceremony, shows the bridal party Bob Wyber, Jean Jack, John Pedersen & Sybil Hunter, poised on the stairs. The camera is focused on the smiling Bride & Groom.

In the back ground are family and friends, and the mother of the bride. Topsy is wearing a short lacy sleeve dress, with a turned up saucer shaped hat topped with silk flowers. She's standing to the right of the church door and looking a little sad with the thought of losing her daughter.

William & Dorothy Pedersen After their marriage, Bill and Dot stayed with Topsy and John, at 11 Clarke Street Berala. Then they rented a house in Dewrang Street Lidcombe before moving in with Nana Roden, at 70 Cambridge Street Lidcombe. Later they bought Nana Roden's place, with an understanding she stayed with them.

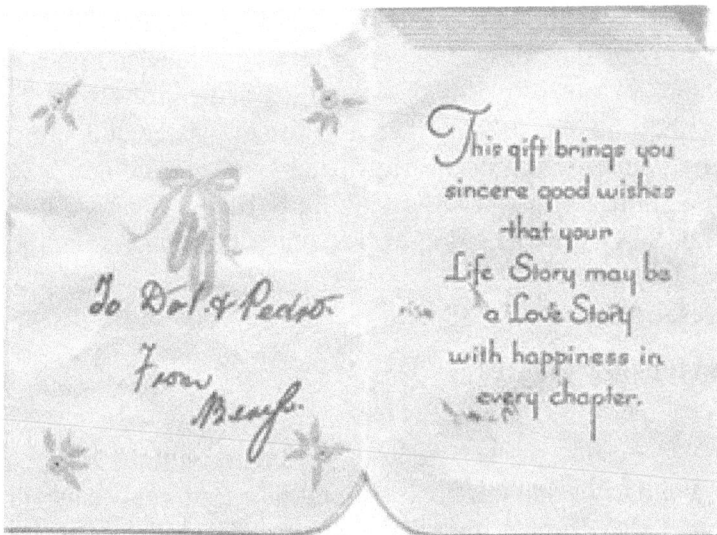

To Dot & Pedro
From Beryl.

This gift brings you
sincere good wishes
that your
Life Story may be
a Love Story
with happiness in
every chapter.

Chapter 12

The enemy within

Though Beryl could walk; she still needed the aid of an Orthopaedic corset. The body brace came up under each arm and down past her waist. While there was no pain, echoing in her mind, was what the doctor's had said: "That one day her spine would collapse and it was inadvisable for her to go to work". So she had to stay at home.

During the day Beryl would sit on the front porch, keeping herself busy knitting and sewing. Seeing the neighbours on their way to work and the kids going to school, she would wave and chat to them as they passed by. As each day comes and goes her dissatisfaction was growing, this wasn't the life she wanted. She wanted the one that her mother and father, sister and brother had. She wanted children, a life of her own and couldn't help feeling a slight twinge of envy looking at their life and wanting the same. So Beryl was going to find out if there was something she could do about it.

The Extension Guides

From 1945 – 1947 Beryl was in the extension guides when she meets Wanda. Wanda had long shining hair that was beautifully styled and she dressed in stylish tailor made clothes that were made to fit her not so perfect body. They became good-friends often spending time together.

Wanda was lucky and unlucky at the same time.

Lucky, because she lived in a nice home in the city with loving parents who were well-off and able to provide her with all the care and support she needed.

Wanda was unlucky though because she had noticeable physical problems. However Wanda had more self-confidence than most able bodied people, she was President of the Orana Club and the lead singer in a band.

Wanda & Beryl

Beryl's Diary, May 1945

May 14th – 19th The Guides had a Handcrafts
Exhibition day

This was another successful day, although a lot
of work was put into it. We were frightfully
busy for weeks before hand making things for
this day; each company had their own stall and
each girl had to stay with the stall for a
certain period, so that no one could touch the
things and tell them what it is etc.

So when it came to my turn to watch the stall
I'd just settled down, when one of the Guiders
came over and told me to give a little present
to Lady Gowrie, well you can imagine how I
felt, I didn't know I had to give her a
present so I didn't have time to rehearse a
speech they told me a few lines to say because
I told them I wasn't much at speech making ,
and I kept saying these lines over and over
again to myself, At last she came over escorted
by a couple of Scouts and Guiders. I just
mumbled something and gave her the present then
away she went, well I just sat down with
relief, I can assure you.

After my turn was done I changed over with
another Guide and went to see what else there
was. It was lovely to see all the things that
were made. Just for a bit of fun we went and
got all the signatures of the Scouts and Guides
we could, so if you are wondering just what all

the scribble on the program is that is what it is.

Ah! but we had fun though running from one section to another and meeting all of our cobbers again, One thing about these gatherings we can see our friends there so that is really makes the day a big success because we don't feel lonely when you see your friends are around you.

I made a "Duchess Set" a cot cover, and helped to make up the Dolls House; each Guide of our Extension Company did a room for the Dolls House, We made them out of butter boxes.

I was given the bathroom and the lavatory to do; at first I didn't know how I was going to go about it, but I remembered what Captain told us "A Guide never says she can't do it; she does it"; so I just did it.

Beryl Wyber playing the Accordon

The
SCOUT and GUIDE
Handcrafts and Hobbies
Exhibition

Lower Town Hall, Sydney

May, 14-19   Price : 6d.

Girl Guides' Association   Boy Scouts' Association
Kelvin House,   Australia House,
15 Castlereagh Street,   38 Carrington Street,
SYDNEY   SYDNEY

Dolls House

Beryl's Diary, June 1945

Although I'm not a Ranger yet I trust it won't
be long before I am one; I've found it most
interesting although the years I've only worked
for 4 badges they being The Knitters, The

Collectors , The Toymakers Badges and a Second Class one.

You, who read this may think "and well she ought to feel guilty she should have a first class badge by this" but unfortunately I've been in hospital and unable to do the things required you see, Our Captain Miss Priddle has formed a Company of crippled and invalid girls and has done a very good job at that, so we only do half of what you active girls do.

We do tracking by the usual way but Morse is sent out a bit different as we all can't stand up so captain made some hand flags for us, then we all know how to hold them then; Captain also arranges outings for us and yes ! Even camp (for those that are able) we went for the first time in 1945 but I'll give you details of that further on in the book.

All our girls are friendly and they are all pals together we go out with each other outside the guide meetings and share each other's confidences, which I think makes an everlasting comradeship.

We do knots, which I like very much; there are lots of things we can do, We miss our Captain very much in summer as that is when she goes to the mountains. But she doesn't let our work lag as she makes up a book with some work in it and post it to a guide then that guide sends it on to another guide and so on then the last guide sends it back to Captain, who corrects work.

Now most of our girls have decided to join the Rangers I am so glad though because that means we will still be together including Captain as she has decided to train so that she can train us then.

August 15th, 1945 the End of World War II

Japan surrenders to the Allies, and ends the Second World War, the day is known as V-P Day (Victory in the Pacific). Now the War was over, her brother Bob was demobbed from the Navy.

Beryl's Diary: 2nd Post Rangers Glengarry Camp 1945

At last we were going on our first camp, just imagine the excitement there was among us; we made arrangements with Captain (she never came with us; but came up the next day with Lady Julius; to see how we were getting on).

I met captain at Strathfield Station where another little girl was waiting too; she was one of Miss Robertson's Blind Company from there we got the train to Town Hall Station we walked over to the Town Hall another Blind Guider named Eva Cooper was waiting for us. Finally our trucks came (there were two) Captain made sure we were all in safely luggage and all, then she left us we drove on to Glengarry where Miss Robertson met us and told us she was to look after us while we were here.

We made our beds and were shown to our rooms; Wanda, Betty, Linda and I shared the one room; we had taps and finally went to sleep, wondering what the morrow would bring forth.

Heaven's Special Mum

Morning! We were awaken by the Blind girls talking up the other end of the veranda, then Miss Robertson came up and told us to get dressed and washed; so we jumped out and did what she bade us to do she warned us that we would have inspection so of course we were awhile getting dressed we were all helping each other. Inspection over we had breakfast then of course we had prayers and colours, then made our beds and washed up. We all had turns at doing the washing up and sweeping and dusting; cleaning the bathroom; lavatory and whatnots.

After that was done we did a bit of tracking and first aid, had lunch, and a rest in bed for a while then went for a walk had tea, had a sing song in a hut because it was raining but we had a lovely log fire; After singing we had some steaming hot cocoa gee! It was good.

The next day was run more or less the same way only after tea we had our camp fire in the opening now it had stopped raining then and some Guiders and Rangers came up from their camp and joined us in a sing song. It was fun; we all went up for some Cocoa

The next day we didn't do much because we were going home and it took us all our time to go through our routine and pack our things up and leave everything how we found it.

Finally Captain came and took up all home and we were all bubbling over with happiness and trying to tell Captain all about it in a short time we had in the car with her; however I don't know what we would have done without Miss Robertson because she was a wonderful help to us all and I think all of the girls would agree if I just said "Thanks, Miss Robertson, You're a darling".

Welcome Rally to their Royal Highnesses the Duke and Duchess of Gloucester

Beryl's Diary. November 10th, 1945

Well this was a very nice day, it would have been if the sun had come out, it was a lovely site to see; I didn't take an active part in it though, it was at the sports ground :Our Guides sat on a few seats besides the Grand Stand, we could see alright and that was the main thing.

First; All the Girl Guides and Guiders and Rangers, Sea Rangers , Scout's, Scout's Masters lined up with their individual flags then the Duke and Duchess of Gloucester arrived, the National Anthem was played while the flags were dipped, in salute. The Duke and Duchess then proceeded to inspect the Scouts and Guides on parade.

The most interesting of the Rally was the Grand March of the Scouts and Guides, it was most colourful that I would have given anything to have had a colour camera with me as it happened one of our girls Betty Maloney, stood up on the seat and took some snaps of the march and tried to get one of the Duke and Duchess as they passed in their car, But she was not very successful much to our sorrow.

Even the cubs and Brownies had a chance to show everyone what they could do.

So as well as having entertainment we got a chance to see it all, of our cobbers that we had made friends with in camp so of course as they went by on floats we gave them encouragement by shouting to them. So all in all we had a very nice day.

In 1946, her brother Bob Wyber attended a University Faculty to study Engineering. He had found his niche in life and perused it with great enthusiasm.

1946 Operation on back

Beryl was eighteen, and staying with a relative in Wollongong when she came across an article in the newspaper... About a young girl, who only 18 months ago, went home from work with a pain in the back, the Doctors had diagnosed; Spinal Tuberculosis. The newspaper went on to say, that the girl had every confidence in an operation which the doctors will soon perform. They propose; to take a piece of bone from her hip and graft it onto her spine.

After the operation, she will spend a considerable time in bed, before an attempt was made to restore the use of her limbs.

After reading this article, Beryl decided to make some enquires regarding the procedure, and went to the Wollongong Hospital. The doctor explained the operation, along with the benefits and risks, and said:

> 'You will be required, to provide written
> consent for the operation to go ahead. ... Beryl
> was keen, so they gave her a form to fill out.'

In those days you weren't legally an adult until you were 21, so the form had to be signed by her mother. While in discussion about the operation, Beryl pressed her mother to sign the form.

However, Topsy was concerned that if it didn't work, she might be worse off, and was unwilling to sign. Beryl thought her

Mother was wrong and decided she wasn't going to let this opportunity slip by, so she forged her mother's signature…

The Hospital's policy was to send a telegram to say when the operation was to go head. It was sometime early in March the telegram was delivered to 11 Clarke Street, when Topsy read the message, she made a frantic dash by train to Wollongong to try and stop it.

By the time Topsy reached the hospital it was too late, all she could do was pray that Beryl would be alright.

Fortunately the operation proved to be successful and the body brace was no longer needed.

In 1946, Beryl became an aunty, when in the month of May her sister Dot and her husband Bill had a baby girl. Then in November of the same year, her brother Bob and his wife Nancýe also had a baby girl. She loved them to bits and couldn't wait to have a baby of her own.

Sometime within that year the family, became the owner of a small Heinz 57 variety dog they called him Skipper. They also acquired a tabby tom cat and called him Billy.

Chapter 13

1945 -1948 'Orana Club'

The word "Orana" is an Aboriginal greeting, translated means 'Welcome.' This organization for the handicapped was opened to disabled persons aged 15 to 30. It was first started by parents and friends in 1944 to help their children re-adjust to everyday life after living so long in hospital.

The room was located in the basement of a building on the corner of Bent and O'Connell Street in Sydney. The Rotary Club helped to furnish and decorated its new headquarters. The Orana Club was run by Miss Jean Garside. Entertainment on Club nights included playing Chess, reading, playing records, film nights and for the more active members a game of ping pong. Those who cannot travel by public transport were driven to the clubroom by Rotarians. In June 1946 the Orana Club held its 2nd birthday celebration dinner and dance night. Beryl was 18 ½ years old and was starting to feel comfortable within the group of over 50 members.

Back row: L to R: Bob, Beryl, Ray, Miss Garside, Nancy, Ray,
Front: June, Wanda, Beryl Wyber, and Rosemary.

Orana 2nd Birthday

Glengarry Camp

Beryl's Diary. October 4th - 7th 1946

Ah! Camp is here again: First of all I went to Strathfield Station and met June (Miss Robertson's Company) and Wanda, then a few minutes later we met Kathleen and Mrs Sealey, finally Captain arrived in her car.

We all scrambled in it while Captain put our luggage in the back, Mrs Sealey was invited to stay in the car and see Glengarry Camp, and Wanda came up with us but came back with Mrs Sealey.

We had soup and sandwiches for tea, then the rest of the girls came later on in the evening including Linda who is now a Guider. The Randwick Rangers cooked for us.

Heaven's Special Mum

We went and had a sing song in the hut and learned a new song called "Music Alone Shall Live", we all went to bed early Miss Robertson was there again to look after us.

Pat Dwyer came with Miss Rooks, Morning! We rose and did our routine work; Miss Bardsly was there; gee! She was fun; she had a wonderful sense of humour. We had flag drill, we being Kath, Pat and myself so that was something else we learned; then low! And behold if we didn't have to see our flag touching the ground because the blind girls were practising the Royal Dip, Kath and myself were pretty nervous watching our flag getting dirty fortunately it didn't get too dirty.

I forgot to mention that Elizabeth came with her mother in the car; Pat went home on Saturday afternoon. We had tea, a sing song, bath, then to bed.

Sunday: Kath, Pat Allen, four Guiders and two blind girls went to church (Catholic). We got up had breakfast washed up; Having morning tea Wanda came up again; so Kath, Pat Allen, Wanda and myself went for a walk and laid a track, Kath screamed because she thought she had walked into a spider web but on investigations found out it was only her hair.

Monday: We went for a walk down to the gully Pat Allen, Kath, Wanda and myself. We got down alright and at the bottom we rested and saw the other guides, playing with little black frogs, about the size of your thumbs.

We thought we'd better get back although the going was twice as bad as going down, however, we finally got back and rested our weary bones then packed our bags and waited for tea; We had sandwiches and milk; Miss Beardsley, looked after us and got us some tea, finally Captain came and took us home there wasn't as much this time as there were last time, seeing that Pat Allen went home with Wanda and another Guider into town.

June, Kath and myself were left in the car we had fun trying to find our way to each place, but finally arrived home in one piece.

Beryl's Diary. November, 1946

Well we have done our test and five of us are going to be enrolled on Saturday the 16th November, am I nervous! We are going to have a party too, so that won't be too bad, the five girls are: Wanda, Kathleen, Pat, Brenda and myself of course. We went on another camp last October, Gee! It was good.

Last Saturday week 26th October was my birthday and Captain gave me a surprise party, she also gave me another surprise by telling me that I have been awarded..."The Badge of Fortitude"...Gee! I was thrilled

PRESIDENT:
HER ROYAL HIGHNESS THE PRINCESS ROYAL.

TELEPHONES: VICTORIA 6001
(4 LINES).

TELEGRAMS: GIRGUIDUS, SOWEST, LONDON.

CODE: 5 LETTER WESTERN UNION.

THE GIRL GUIDES ASSOCIATION.

(INCORPORATED BY ROYAL CHARTER)

IMPERIAL HEADQUARTERS:

17-19, BUCKINGHAM PALACE ROAD,

LONDON, S.W.1.

21st October, 1946.

Dear Beryl,

I have very great pleasure in sending you the Badge
of Fortitude which the Imperial Executive has awarded
you in proud recognition of the great courage you have
shown during your illness.

The Overseas Committee would like to join with the
Executive in sending you their warm congratulations.
We do know that not only the Guides in Australia but all
Guides here too will feel glad pride when they read of
your award.

Yours sincerely,

Charlotte Cooper.

(Lady Cooper.)

Commissioner for Guiding in the Empire Overseas.

Post Ranger Beryl Wyber,

The Dude Ranch

In the summer of 1947, the Orana Club organized a Camp, at the John Frances 'Dude Ranch' in Castlereagh Road. Travelling by train from the city it was a one and a half hour journey to the ranch which was located at the foot of the Blue Mountains. The Dude Ranch sat on 36 acres, with extensive frontage to the Nepean River. There were 40 cabin style bedrooms with bath and shower rooms, meals were served daily in the dining room consisting of fresh vegetables, pork, poultry, fresh cream and milk.

Every night, there was entertainment of dancing to a seven piece orchestra on a spacious dance floor.

Every day, the cowboys show off their horse riding skills with a Rodeo. The more adventurous learnt how to ride on selected good natured horses.

Day time activities also include swimming in the Nepean River, snooker on a full sized billiard table, tennis, hiking, and hay ride. In true cowboy style, pictures show the mode of transport was a small pick-up truck crammed with eleven or more people piled in the back sitting down and hanging on tight. There was also a hiking trip up Mitchell Pass, on the completion of the climb to Elizabeth Lookout they had a magnificent view of the Cumberland Plain, a nurse was always in attendance on all the outings.

During that holiday the soldiers organized a moonlight cruise on the Nepean River in medium sized boats with outboard motors, making for an uncomfortable ride. Holiday snapshots show a hint of romance when Beryl meet a man named Ray.

The Dude Ranch campers
Front sixth from the left: Beryl Wyber

February 1947; after summer camp, Beryl and Wanda met up at Bankstown Baths, with conversations recalling some of the events that took place at the ranch.

The time, when Ray got down on hands and knees pretending to be a bucking bronco, while Beryl played a cow girl riding on his back while waving her cow girl-hat in the air.

Sharing her feelings, she told Wanda how Ray had put his arm around her on the moonlight cruise which made her heart flutter. They giggled about the boys folding their arms pushing their biceps out to impress the girls. Lazing around the pool they chatted away until the day slipped away.

Ray & Beryl

News: Walked in Secret

http://nla.gov.au/nla.news-page1004579

Beryl Wyber was in Royal Prince Alfred Hospital for 10 ½ years with a spinal injury that meant she would never walk.

Convinced she could walk, if only she tried, Beryl slipped out of bed every night when the lights were out and practised. Only when she could walk the length of the bed did she tell the doctors and nurses what she had been doing.

Now Beryl is out of hospital, walking. At a ceremony in the St James Hall, Phillip Street, next Sunday, she will receive the Guides Badge of Fortitude for her courage.[24]

---

[24] *The Sydney Morning Herald Wednesday 26 February 1947, page 1, 5*

EXTENSION GUIDES' OWN.

Sunday, 2nd March, 1947 at 3 p.m.

HYMN: "Brightly gleams our Banner".

All remain standing for entry of the Flags.

The Lord's Prayer

The Lesson

The Dedication of the World Flag

The Guide Prayer

HYMN: "I would be true"

THE ADDRESS: Rev. W.G. Nisbet.

HYMN: "Open my eyes"

Presentation of Badge of Fortitude by Lady Julius
Chief Commissioner, N.S.W.,
to
Post Ranger, Beryl Wyber.

The Guide Promise .. led by .. Lady Julius.

HYMN: "My faith"

NATIONAL   ANTHEM.

----oOo----

The Presentation of the Badge of Fortitude Programme

Beryl's Diary. March, 1947

Well! We were enrolled by Miss Merle Dear, and everything went off very nicely. All our mothers were there, so that made it a lot nicer.

I was presented with my Badge of Fortitude, on the 2nd instant, by Lady Julius, Chief Commissioner for N.S.W at a Guide's Own, in St James, Hall in Phillip Street, Sydney; The Rev. Nesbit gave the service.

1947 Beryl, Betty & Helen

GIRL GUIDES ASSOCIATION
(N.S.W. Branch)

15 CASTLEREAGH STREET
SYDNEY

TELEPHONES:
B4625   BW3794

State Commissioner:
LADY JULIUS

State Secretary:
MISS L. MITCHELL

4th March, 1947.

Dear Beryl,

All Brownies, Rangers, Guides and Guiders of the Extension Branch congratulate you on the spirit shown by you, for which the Badge of Fortitude was presented to you last Sunday. We are happy that you received such recognition, knowing you will always keep up that spirit.

Yours sincerely
Beryl Rooke
Extension Secretary.

GIRL GUIDES ASSOCIATION
Congratulation letter
Dear Beryl

*All Brownies Rangers, Guides and Guides of the Extension
Branch congratulate you on the spirit show by you and for
which the Badge of Fortitude was presented to you last Sunday.*

*We are happy that you received such recognition knowing you
will always keep up that spirit.*
Yours sincerely
Beryl Rooke

Extension Secretary

March 15th, 1947

With a winsome-smile, Beryl posed for her portrait.

Seated on a wooden chair hands coupled together with The
Badge of Fortitude pinned onto the right hand side of Beryl's
uniform, the reporter clicked the camera shutter.
The black and white photo is for the newspaper - to tell her
story.
Later - Beryl jokingly said:
> 'I thought I looked like the Mona Lisa sitting on
> that chair.'

Out of the many photos' I have of my mother this the one photo
I cherish the most. It's the one I look at each day and the one
that has been an inspiration to me throughout my life.

112

The interview for the Newspapers:

Legg: When did you receive this award, Beryl?

Beryl: A fortnight ago,- it was presented to me at a 'Guides Own' at the St James Hall in Phillip Street, by Lady Julius, Chief Commissioner for Guides in NSW.

Legg: And is this the first Fortitude Award in Australia?

Beryl: I don't think so – but it's the first in New South Wales.

Legg: Well now, will you tell us what you received the award for?

Beryl: Well, officially it's for Fortitude under suffering – and I got it for being a patient in hospital.

Leg: Tell us something about your time in hospital? – How long were you there?

Beryl: I was in hospital for 12 years.

Legg: Gosh! And how old were you when you went in, Beryl.

Beryl: I went in when I was a year and five months and came out when I was 13.

Legg: And you had a spinal injury, did you?

Beryl: Yes - it seems I fell out of my pram – and after a week or two, mum found a lump on my back, she took me to hospital, and the doctors said I had a T.B. spine.

Legg: And they kept you in hospital, did they?

Beryl: Yes – the doctors kept on saying I could go home in a few months – but they kept on keeping me there for a few months more.

Legg: And I suppose you had to keep perfectly still?

Beryl: I was supposed to. The doctors and nurses kept telling me to, but I wouldn't and then I'd get put in the baby's ward as punishment.

Legg: And were you ever completely paralysed?

Beryl: No – I could always move my arms and legs – though I wasn't supposed to, they used to strap me down, but I'd undo the straps.

Legg: Why – through sheer naughtiness?

Beryl: No – I felt if I didn't use my muscles they'd become useless, I was kept in plaster for a time but I'd get up at night and move around, then after 12 years in hospital the doctors said I could try walking; They thought it would take me a month to learn – and they were quite surprised when I just got up and went home – surrounded by newspaper reporters.

Legg: That must have been a good moment – and then you've been all right ever since, have you?

Beryl: Oh no, exactly a year later, on the anniversary of the day I left hospital, I was back again with meningitis.

Legg: Good heavens! And how long did that last?

Beryl; Oh! About three months.

Legg: And was it very bad?

Beryl: The worst part was the needles – they used to inject into the small of my back. I didn't have an anaesthetic and they said: I was plucky, but I did a bit of yelling all the same.

Legg: And then you were cured of that, were you?

Beryl: Yes, I went to school and then to business college.

Legg: And was your spine all right?

Beryl: Well, I didn't have any pain , but the doctors said my spine would collapse one day, so about a year ago, I went back to hospital for an operation, they grafted a piece of bone from my hip onto my spine.

Legg: And now you're perfectly all right?
Beryl: Yes – everything's just okey - dokey. I don't have to have any support at all and I go to work like everyone else.

Legg: And what work are you doing, Beryl?
Beryl: I work at the Girl Guides Association – it's my first job and I've been in it for more than a week now. They're very good to me there and I enjoy myself immensely. After years of being told: "You shouldn't go to work – you're not strong enough yet "– it's wonderful to have a job.

Chapter 14

Skeet

Reginald James Rae; was born in Toongabbie 27th April, 1929. He had a nick-name, his father called him Skeeter. He thinks it was short for mosquito, because he was small for his age and always buzzing around somewhere, from then on the name stuck.

Skeet was short in stature, his habit of smoking had started early in his life behind the school shed. He led an active life, riding his bike, swimming, playing football with his mates for North Manly. As a result of his physical activities he had developed a fine physique.

His hair, once fair and unruly was now well-groomed dark-brown and wavy. Once freckled faced and shunned by the girls in school, he was now a good looking bloke with a cheeky grin and soft nature.

The girls had changed their opinion about him and he had changed his opinion about them.

On 25th April 1945, just two days before his sixteenth birthday, Skeet had just started working as a Storeman for Distributors of Wholesale Groceries, he had been working there loading and unloading the trucks and that's when he became ill. Taken to The Prince Henry Coast Hospital, they confirmed that he had contracted Poliomyelitis; a viral infection which can lead to paralysis of the arms, legs or the diaphragm.

The conventional treatment at the time involved imposing strict immobilization, during the acute and convalescent phases with standardized splints and Bradford frames to which you were strapped on boards, sometimes for months.

They put him into an isolation ward and there on his own, he was laid out on his back in bed.

They tied both his arms up at the elbows to the back of the bed, but he felt no pain except for when the doctor sent a needle into his spine.

This was for the purpose of taking fluid samples and testing for meningitis, the results confirmed that it was Polio.

Each day the nurse came around and checked his bowel motions, if you didn't go you had to take a pill, if you still didn't go, you had to take castor oil mixed with orange juice. If you still didn't go, you were woken up about 4 am and given an enema.

He was in the Isolation ward, where he had to lie on his back and he couldn't get his hands to meet. With no one to talk to no wireless to listen to, his arms tied to the back of the bed he couldn't even read. All he could do was contemplate his future, which at that time seemed very grim at that time, he wished he could finish it right there and then.

When these moods came over him to take his mind off it, he would sing, but then he started to think of others he had seen being pushed around in a wheelchair and the black moods returned.

Looking out the window he could only see a brick wall, a little Chinese Nurse named Quong came in and said: "look at the view"! He said: "Yes it's a brick wall." So she turned his bed around and held him up so he could see the Golf Course and the Coastline. But he was getting a bit mad about it all, especially when they said he couldn't walk.

He said: "He was sick of being tied up like this and he wanted to get out of there." The nurse said: "What for? You couldn't walk anyway; you can't even get out of bed."

He thought I walked in here and I can walk out! He had made up his mind - he was getting out somehow so he got out of these things that had him bound up.

He swung his legs over the bed and went to sit up and found he couldn't, he was balancing on the side of the bed his body was stiff as a board his muscles pulling and hurting. After all attempts to get in or out of bed failed, it finished up he had to sing out for help, because he was stuck he couldn't go forward and he couldn't go backwards.

For the first time in his life, he felt real fear.

And no one could tell him whether he would be able to walk again, or if he was to be confined to a bed or wheel chair, or even worse than that, on his back being hand feed by the nurses.

Over the next three weeks different doctors examined him and they decided to put him in a frame. His legs were strapped eighteen inches apart; his chest was strapped and with his arms tied up in the air.

Skeet told his mother he wasn't having any bloody frames. He remembered six years ago when his older brother Bill then aged fourteen had Polio, and the entire family was in quarantine for three weeks. He thought the only thing good about that was he had time off from school.

119

Bill had been strapped up; and it hadn't done him any good. Later Bill was transferred to the Sister Kenny Clinic where he was in hospital for about two years. When he left hospital his spine was badly curved and one leg waisted. But he did come out walking, without the help of crutches or any other support.

Skeet wanted the Sister Kenny treatment.

Skeet's mother made sure he was transferred to The Sister Kenny Clinic in the Royal North Shore Hospital where he was put in the 'Carey Ward' located on the ground floor. The 'Dibbs Ward' was the Woman's ward located above. His bed was on an open veranda with large blinds that dropped down in bad weather.

The Sister Kenny's treatment:

Skeet was wheeled down each day for treatment, bed and all from the ward and returned each evening. While he was there they got blanket strips and put them in boiling water taken out with tongs. They put the blanket strips through a hand wringer then wrapped them around the affected parts of the body.

In his case they were the right shoulder to the elbow and the right hip to the knee. They kept doing that for a while to loosen up his muscles. Normally it would have burned you but it didn't because the muscles were too tight to feel anything. The physio would then bend his joints until it hurt. This went on for about two months until he could feel the heat of the hot packs and his joints could be bent normally with little pain.

He was laid in an extra-large bath were he could extend his arms sideways with the help of the hot water, and then onto a table for more exercises.

After some time when he could sit up on his own, after exercises he would sit at one end of the bath, while they attached the hose to the cold water tap then they would turn on the water and spray up and down his spine until he turned pink and purple.

When he stopped screaming the other kids came around the screen to have a look and started laughing. He looked like a drowned rat. He was told the reason for the spray was to get the circulation moving, all he knew was that it was dammed cold. Thankfully at the end of each session they did put him back into a warm bath to warm him up before they lifted him out.

Everyone had to drink a glass of milk each day. He was lying on a table which was parallel with the bath, when the milk was handed out. Looking to his right he noticed a hand turned over and pouring the milk down the sink. He said: "What's going on here?" Little Richard's head came around the screen with a frown on his forehead and one finger on his lips. Skeet didn't know if the sister knew - but no one ever squealed on him.

Skeet didn't make it home for Christmas that year and was there for about ten months. But eventually he was one of the lucky ones that did. When he could walk around, his right arm still hung at his side.

When it came to walking up steps he had to place his left foot on the step above and lift his right leg up to meet his left.

Going down steps he would place his right foot down then bring his left foot down to meet it, if he had his left foot off the ground and his right knee was only slightly bent he would fall over and it was a heck of a job to get up again.

A bloke by the name of Joe Smith from Kensington was two doors up in another room and there was also a bloke named Kelly from La Perouse in the bed next to him. Joe and Skeet got into a bit of trouble once when another kid came in and left him his clothes. Skeet knew Joe had some clothes in his locker so he said to Joe how about we go to the Picture's tonight. Joe replied ok as he was keen to go.

Skeet was just on his feet at that time and still a bit unsteady but they both went off to the Pictures. Skeet's trousers he borrowed were up around his ankles and the shirt sleeves were a bit short on him. Joe - well he had two dropped feet and he had to lift his legs up high because his toes touched the ground first.

So off they went - they caught the tram up the hill for about two stops before walking into The North Sydney Cinema in Miller Street and purchased the tickets for the movie.

They had hoped that the nurse wouldn't report them after returning to the hospital from the show and felt sure they wouldn't put them in, since they got on well with them. They watched the show - when the Movie finished Joe as usual was first out high stepping because of his floppy feet. By the time Skeet got out there, he could see Joe standing between two big chaps in suits. Skeet was standing on the top of the stairs and asked: "What's up Joe"

One of the gentlemen standing with him looked at Skeet and said to Joe. 'Where's your mate?' Joe said: "Inside". So he wouldn't make a liar out of him Skeet just walked straight out the door and took off down the road. It was a cold night and Skeet had to walk a reasonable half hour distance back to the Hospital before climbing through a hole in the paling fence and getting back into bed.

But what they both didn't know was a new nurse had been transferred to the ward that night and had noted their absence in the report book. When Skeet got there his bed was stripped, therefore he had to report to the nurse and ask why his bed was stripped. The night nurse said: "Oh" so she arranged to have his bed made up and Skeet got into it.

The next thing, Joe comes in. Skeet said: "What happened to you?" He said: "I came back in the police car - they run me home." Skeet said: "You rotten mongrel". He was dirty because he had to walk home, then while the nurse was making his bed she asked how Skeet liked the movie - then said: "I like to see someone with a bit of go in them, to stir the place up for a while."

The next day Skeet asked Joe what the Police said. He told Skeet one of them asked what his name was. When he said: "Joe Smith' they called me a bloody liar." Joe also got into some trouble from the nurse. She went him because he was the leader of the bunch and also for taking Skeet with him. Joe tried to convince her that it was Skeet's suggestion.

Joe said: "Skeet was the leader of the bunch - he was the one that suggested it." Skeet said: "Suggested what - Joe." But he had no hope, when he looked over at Skeet for support; Skeet had just put on a sweet innocent look.

Skeet thought - that will teach you to leave me stranded at the bottom of the ramp in a wheelchair the night you nearly ran into the matron and the superintendent.
The Police went out to inform the mothers - when his Eileen and Mrs Smith came down to the Hospital they had to face the Superintendent. Skeet didn't know much of what was going on, however when his mum came around she said: "Poor Mrs

123

Smith", when she got in there he gave her what-O! and she came out nearly in tears.

Eileen went in and as always, her best form of defence was attack so she started on them.

> "They had let her 16 year old boy who was handicapped go out - he could have fallen under a bus or anything!
> You left clothes around were he could get them!
> I'm going to contact the Mirror and The Daily Telegraph Newspapers about this.

Hearing the commotion: The Superintendent came right down and assured Eileen that it wouldn't happen again.

When Eileen left the office she went straight over to see Skeet. She told him about all the trouble he caused her, of having to leave home early so now she'd have to go home and catch up and prepare dinner for the rest of the family when they arrive home from work.

After telling Skeet this Eileen said to him: "Don't you do that again to me you bugger." Skeet said: "No Mum."

Skeet was one of the lucky ones that did come out of hospital in 1946, sometime after Christmas.

Chapter 15

Number 9 Boots

Skeet had trouble lifting his right arm above his head, it still hung by his side, and he couldn't move his right leg freely either. But he was glad to be away from the hospital, and getting around despite the handicap. He was an outpatient for some time. Social Security paid him five shillings a week sickness benefits, which was only enough to catch a bus each week to the clinic for therapy. He had to rely on his parents to feed and clothe him.

That's when he also had a lot of trouble going around trying to get a job. No one would employ him. He had sort of given up, but he did learn not to give up and found someone was always there to help, if you are willing to try. He had trouble with every day basic jobs, like ironing his shirt; he would take hold of the iron handle but didn't have the strength to push the damn thing. He would take hold of his right hand with his left and *fling* it away and wished it was cut off then it couldn't get in the way, but he didn't have the courage to do so.

Later he was glad he didn't cut it off, because it had come in handy since then. He was in one of those dark moods, when he saw the doctor at the clinic. The doctor listened to Skeet with what he had to say, about not being able to work and pull his weight like the rest of the family. He couldn't join in activities and had to come to the Clinic each day.

Then the doctor gave him some advice that he never forgot.

He said: "Put on your number 9 boots turn yourself around and give yourself a good kick up the rear end!"
Skeet was surprised at what he said, but it made him think:

> "What am I going to do? Sit down cry like a baby and whine about my troubles and bore everyone to death. Or put my best foot forward and do something about improving my situation."

He started going to Harbord baths, through the middle of the week, so as no one would see him because he felt self-conscious and sensitive of the wastage in his arm and leg. Slowly he could swim again and ride his push bike.

Hanging around Manly War Memorial where they held dances, Skeet meet up with a teenager about his own age, his name was Johnny Bennett, and it was a friendship that lasted for a number of years. Johnny was a good looking man, had dark wavy hair with a disarming smile. He also had Osteoporosis in the leg and was getting around with a walking stick. Already a member of the Orana Club, he asked Skeet to come along to a meeting.

Johnny Bennett, Skeet & Beryl

The Orana Club

Skeet was almost 18, he found they were a happy group and felt at ease among them. These people never looked at you as if you were handicapped as they would laugh at the fumbles and help each other, so he continued to go along to the Saturday night meetings.

127

Around this time Beryl was 19 years old, had a bubby personality, thick shoulder length auburn hair that had natural tight waves framing her oval face and she had noticed Skeet.

The Royal National Park

The Orana club went by train to The Royal National Park, just outside of Sydney for a picnic; a whole group of them.

While they were there, one chap, seem to have some sort of problem with his leg although he didn't need crutches or a walking stick to get around decided that he would have a wrestle with Skeet. So they started to wrestle and he was on top of Skeet, and he had him pinned down on the ground.

Skeet could have tossed him off. But he was screaming out! "Watch out for that leg, don't hurt that leg."

Skeet didn't know which one, so he was lying there with him on top and he was trying to figure out which leg it was, when...

Beryl threw sand into the other chap's face, he got up quickly trying to get the sand out of his eyes and at the same time going crook. Someone said to Beryl: "You shouldn't have done that!" She was feeling a bit embarrassed and moved away from the group and stood aloof and alone, Skeet felt sorry for her and went over and said:

> "It's alright. I could have tossed him off, and you shouldn't really have done it. I was just worried about his leg and wasn't sure what was wrong with it."

Beryl got a bit upset, and Skeet said: "Never mind... don't worry she'll be right."

The Train Ride home

It was plain as the nose on your face that Beryl was sweet on Skeet. Therefore Wanda contrived a plan to bring them together, and everyone was in on it. Going back home they were all aboard the crowded train when Wanda with a straight face said to Skeet: "Oh! Where's Beryl?"

Skeet said: "Oh! I don't know! She's probably in one of the other carriages with the rest of them." Wanda said: "Well you'd better go and find her; we've got to get her back!"
Skeet said: "Me!" Wanda said: "Yes you! Go and find her! We'll mind your seat."
Skeet said: "Oh Yeah" ....thinking here we go."

So he starts searching through the carriages and found her two carriages behind, on her own. Skeet said: "What are you doing back here?" Beryl said: "I got lost in the crowd, I couldn't see them." Skeet said:

> "Come on we'll go back with the others. When the train stops at the next station we'll hop out and run back up to the other carriage."

When they reached the next station and the train stopped, they hopped off and ran the two carriages to get back on board. Once back in the carriage two club members got up from minding their seats. Skeet sat in the seat next to the window and Beryl sat down beside him. Skeet thought something's going on here, but he wasn't sure. The others were watching, and said: "What's up

Skeet, what are you thinking about." Skeet said: "Nothing... not a thing everything is alright."

The Royal National Park Picnic 1947

Beryl Wyber

*Reg Rae
(Skeet)*

Chapter 16

Introduction to the Rae family

Beryl and Skeet had been together for some time, when he bought her home to meet the Family and Wanda came along too. They lived at 37 Albert Street in Harbord, in a semi-detached double front weatherboard house. Entering the front door they were on an enclosed veranda. To the right at the end of the veranda is where Skeet and his brother Alf slept.

They entered the inner front door, onto a polished linoleum floor and the hall way. Skeet was greeted by his small crossbreed black/tan Kelpie dog named Henry. Henry has come skidding sideways through the house via the back-door Eileen chases him out the front-door. On the right are two bedrooms, further on is the kitchen, beyond that the lounge room. Out the back door is another enclosed veranda making a third bedroom for Skeet's brothers Bill and Jack, the bathroom is located at the other end of the veranda.

Skeet's father William Robert Livingston Rae was born in 1883, his friends and family called him Bill.
Bill's father Livingston Lawrence Rae born in 1843 was a hard seafaring man of Scottish heritage.

At 64, Bill stands around 5ft 5. His body is lean and wiry, his handsome face tells of a hard and disciplined life. His salt and pepper coloured hair is straight and unstylish, with a home cut short back and sides. His family and friends know him, as a man of high moral principals' who lives his life by the "Ten Commandments".

He doesn't say much, but when he does you could always trust that he is telling you the truth.

He had worked on various jobs over his life time, The Sydney Wharfs with Alf, The Quarries, and various Government jobs.

In his spare time, he would carry the old hand-push lawn-mower and shears over to Queenscliff where the rich people lived, and mow their lawns for two shillings. If the family were lucky, he'd bring home an apple-pie if they were cooking them.

His mother Eileen born in 1895, was 52, wore eye glasses and was around the same height as her husband. She earned extra money cleaning house and washing for a Mrs Fox at Balgowlah.

Her face shows the lines of her age, and her body had lost its womanly charms after having so many children. Her fine greyish hair had a slight wave and was cut short. She came from a large family of eight, by nature she loved to argue and would argue that black was white and white was black just for the fun of it.

Eileen's children all had a Catholic education. In raising them she had learnt a certain amount of psychology and along with the fear of God which she used often, it kept them in line.

She had been married once before and had two other children named Alf and Ernest. They were brothers, to Alice Joyce, who preferred to be called Joyce, Dorothy, Bill, Jack, and Skeet who was the youngest in the family. His mother affectionately called Skeet 'My Baby'.

Both Wanda and Beryl had physical problems, however Wanda's was more apparent and the tailor-made clothes couldn't hide her imperfections.

Eileen just didn't know how to cope when she meet them. In those days everyone felt pressured to have beautiful well dressed and smart children. If you were poor, you didn't want to look like it. Like a lioness protecting her cub she couldn't help it, when she made them feel unwelcome and said: "Anyone would think this was the crippled children's home." Once Eileen was alone with her son, she said:

> "If you did marry Beryl, she will want to have
> two or three kids and because she is not strong,
> she could die and... I will have to look after them".

This was her argument against Beryl. Eileen became further alarmed, when she found out that Beryl had suffered from Tuberculosis. It was in fear that Skeet might catch TB that drove Eileen to urge him to break it off! so they broke up. Skeet began to hang out with the boys he once knew. But he was soon unhappy, because it just wasn't the same any more. They had girlfriends now and he felt out of place.

At home, Beryl was getting snappy and so was Skeet that lasted for about a fortnight. Eileen was still the wedge between them, and continued voicing her objections of disapproval of their relationship.

But Beryl wasn't afraid to speak her mind. So she approached Eileen and said: "why don't you want me to see your son?'

Forced to confront her, Eileen said: "It was because, she had Tuberculosis and went on to explain, that she was worried that she could pass it on to Skeet." Beryl said: "If I thought... that I would give him TB, I'd walk away right now. I would never ever, want to harm him."

Skeet's sister Dorothy, with a sympathetic vote, later suggested they see a specialist to find out if it was a problem. So together, they went to the Macquarie Street Specialist in Sydney. The Specialist said:

> "Tuberculosis is a contagious disease. Like the common cold, it spreads through the air. Only people who are sick with TB in their lungs are infectious, and he told them that there was no way she could give Skeet TB."

Coming home, Skeet was in such high spirits that he was almost dancing down the street. He wanted to tell everyone. Now with Eileen's argument undermined, there was nothing more she could do or say to bring an end to this relationship.

Royal Easter Show March 29th, 1947

Skeet almost 18; was working at the Village Dry Cleaners in Manly, at the end of the week he gave his wages to his mum. Eileen gave him spending money for the week, but that didn't help when he needed to have some extra cash. Beryl and Wanda wanted to go to The Royal Easter Show, so they talked Johnny Bennett and Skeet into going with them. However he couldn't save up anything, so he had to ask his mum for more money to go to the show.

Beryl confronted her and said: "Why don't you give him more money; because he is always broke" Eileen said: "Well I now know that you are after my son and not just his money because he hasn't got any; so if you really like him you'll stick around."

The Classic 1926 Essex

Skeet had his license. His brother in-law Bert (who married his sister Joyce) good-naturedly decided to lend Skeet his Classic 1926 Essex car, so he could take Beryl for a run. As they were driving through the back streets of Curl Curl, Beryl was laughing over some funny comics in the paper and telling Skeet. Skeet didn't quite catch what was said and momentarily took his eyes off the road, when he asked: "What did you say?"

As he turned his head he bought the car over at the same time, looking back to the road there was a post straight in front of them. Skeet swerved to miss the post; it went over the gutter then rolled down the bank.

The Classic 1926 Essex ended upside down on the canvas hood. Skeet and Beryl were alright but shaken by the experience. Some people from across the road let them use the phone to get a message to Bert. Skeet told Bert that he had a bit of an accident with the car and it's not going too well. He let him know where they were and they waited for him to arrive.

Bert arrived with a couple of spanners, only to see the first car he had ever owned overturned with the wheels in the air, crushed roof, smashed windscreen and some paint damage! It was understandable that he was momentary upset; once he cooled down they rolled the car back over onto its wheels again.

At the time a farmer visiting his friends there, said: "I've got a windscreen for a 26 Essex down the garage. I'll send it and you can just pay me for the postage." Skeet was grateful and said: thank you very much for that. In the meantime - Bert had found another windscreen and made him pay for that one too (which meant he had even less pocket money).

Skeet then had to buy the canvas, and make a new hood for the 26 Essex. Painstakingly they pulled the damaged hood off the car, so they had a pattern to work from.

They used a large industrial sewing machine with the heavy duty sewing needle, by the time it was finished it looked like new.

Beryl felt a little guilty and half responsible for distracting Skeet from driving the car that day.
So every week-end she was there while they worked on the car. It was getting a bit monotonous though, and Skeet said: "she needn't hang around" but she still kept coming, because she wanted to be with Skeet.
Finally the car was finished, now they had the weekends free to be with their friends.

Week Ends

With the trauma of the car accident now behind them, from now on their time was their own. A weekend at the Blue Mountains, picnics with the Orana Club, games of cricket and the good times rolled on. They were carefree and as long as they were together, that is the way they wanted it to stay forever.
Catching the train, they went with their friends to Casula Park on the Georges River, where they enjoyed a picnic lunch and having fun was compulsory. The boys Johnny, Albert and Skeet had a few beers and clowned around, while the girls Beryl, Wanda, Stefanie and Shirley joined in the fun and laughed along with them. Happy snaps show Beryl and Skeet totally wrapped

up in each other's arms, with radiant smiles showing the dark and lonely days of the past were gone.

Harbour Cruise

Someone, they knew, had a small motor boat. It was suggested, they all go for a Harbour Cruise for a seaside view of Fort Denison, Luna Park, and the Sydney Harbour Bridge.

Of the eleven photos taken that day, of the group of nine with a box brownie camera, one photo shows; Skeet and Beryl dressed casually, faces touching, their hair wind-blown and looking into the camera with radiant smiles, showing their enjoyment of the day.

Heaven's Special Mum

Skeet & Beryl on the Harbour Cruise

front row middle Beryl holding Box Brownie Camera
Back row far right Skeet

Chapter 17

Harbord Catholic School

When Skeet was younger, he had attended Harbord Catholic School, and although he was never a brilliant scholar, it was just that he wasn't interested. His older sisters and brothers were far in advance of him, and it gave him a bit of a complex. He never did finish school and left early. He had started working around the age of thirteen and a half, for Bert Myers on the bread Carts delivering bread. Giving that away for a while, he then worked for Danny Inskip as a blacksmith striker.

But his day dreams were to go to the country, to become a roustabout, to live the life of a drover, and to be a shearer in the sheds. His mother Eileen wasn't too impressed with the tales going around, of how the drovers and shearers lifestyle was to go into town, blow their cheques at the local pub, and get into fights. So as to not upset his mother, Skeet didn't go.
Since then, he'd found work in the dry cleaners.

In contrast Beryl's brother Bob had his head in the books, studying hard. Bob had completed his 2nd year examination in the Faculty of Engineering Physics, with 11 passes, Distinctions and Credits. Despite Bob's abilities and high intelligence, he was a very unassuming man. One that was good to his mother, and was well thought of and liked by everyone who knew him, and that included Skeet. Although he felt no malice toward Skeet, both Bob and his mother were against the marriage.

They were both concerned, that because Beryl wasn't strong physically. She needed someone, who could not only take care of her financially, but could carry the extra burden, of future health problems. Bob was looking out for his little sister, as well as backing his mother when he said to Beryl: "I don't think it's a good idea for you to get married to Skeet. He doesn't have a stable or well-paying job."

In fact at the time he didn't have a job at all. Beryl's answer to her brother was: "He'll get one."

There was nothing any one could do, or say, that would change her mind. She had given her heart to Skeet, and was eager to marry him, and keen to have a family of her own. Leading up to her desires to marry it seems that every year, someone in the family was getting married, and by now except for Skeet's brother Jack, were all married –

- Beryl's brother, William 1935
- Skeet's sister, Joyce 1943
- Beryl's sister, Dot 1944
- Beryl's brother, Bob 1946
- Skeet's sister, Dorothy 1947
- Skeet's brother, Alf 1948

3 Nieces and 1 Nephew

In the summer of 1948, her brother Bob and sister in-law Nancye had their second child, a boy. Then four months later, her sister Dot and brother-in-law Bill also had another baby girl.

She had three nieces and a nephew, and Beryl was anxious to start her own family, and didn't want to wait much longer.

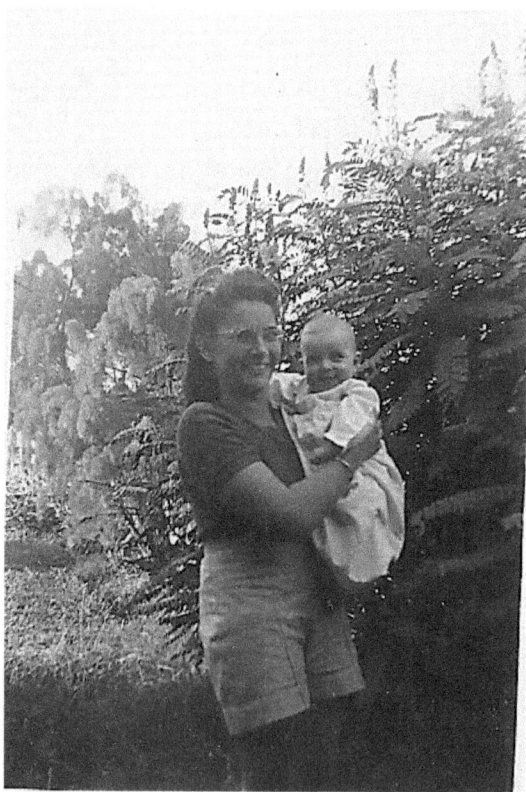

Beryl Wyber & Susan Wyber

Chapter 18

July 1948 'Burradoo'

Topsy and John had talked it over, they were going into partnership with John's brother Bill and his wife Dot. They had decided to run a guest house, not just any guest house this was one of the best.

'Laurel Park' homestead originally built in 1889, by the Hon John Macintosh; was a well-established and exclusive guest house, located on the corner of Moss Vale and Osborne Roads in Burradoo. This beautiful home was situated on almost four acres with park-like gardens, century old trees and exotic shrubs creating an atmosphere of peace, tranquillity and total privacy. On the grounds there was a Tennis court, croquet lawn and a swimming pool.

The slate roofed brick and cement rendered two story home, was built in the traditional style. This fine residence reflecting the era of gracious living with old marble fireplaces complemented by magnificent timberwork of polished cedar, cast iron baths and was one of the finest estates in the Southern Highlands. It had first glass accommodation with 15 bedrooms, and could cater for 35 guests.

They would also cater for afternoon tea and dinner; Topsy would do the cooking, while John would help in the kitchen, as well as order and buy the food needed to run the guest house. John's, Brother Bill would be in charge of the daily running of the house and grounds, while his wife Dot would look after the hospitably and booking office.

So, they sold their home in 11 Clarke Street. Packed up and moved down the South Coast into the Hinterlands, and Beryl had to go with them. It was 65 miles away from her friends, and a life where she was happy. She missed Skeet, so they used to write letters. But that wasn't good enough, and they were both miserable.

So Beryl come back, and lived with Aunt Martha (Topsy's sister) and Uncle John Jack at 58 Moore St, Leichhardt, Sydney. They lived above a shop, and Uncle 'Jack Jack', use to look after the tennis courts at the back of the shops.

Beryl found a job, working at Bennett & Wood Pty Ltd, manufactures of Speedwell Cycles and spare parts. She worked in the office as a Comptometer Operator, making up the bills and posting them to their debtors. Skeet was working at Little's dry cleaners at that time, and use to come and visit her at work.

The Engagement Ring

Beryl and Skeet were to be married. There was one small problem, Beryl wanted an engagement ring. At the time, Skeet was working at the dry cleaners earning a weekly wage of around £9, and he was a little embarrassed, because he didn't know how he was going to afford one. His sister Dorothy said:

"There is a clear cut stone called a cubic zirconia, it looks like a diamond, and no one can tell the difference, would she be satisfied with that?"

So they decide to have a look. They meet up in the heart of the City, and then walked to 'The Strand Arcade.' Built in 1891 and opened in 1892, the style of the building was of grandeur and elegance, highlighted with a tinted glass roof and old world charm. At that time the jewellery shop was located on the ground floor.

They went in. Gazing at the assortment of dazzling diamond rings, displayed in the glass case. The prices ranged from £25 to £75. Next to them were the wedding rings, priced around 55/- to £27. The owner of the shop a fair haired lady named Florence asked, if she could help them. Asking to see the zirconia rings, Florence displayed their assortment. The prices marked on the white Zirconia rings were around £9.

Beryl found one she liked, and put it on her engagement finger. Beryl said: "How does it look?" The shop assistant said: "It looks lovely is it an engagement ring?" Beryl said: "Yeah!"

Now… they were officially engaged. Beryl was blissfully happy, and showed every one the ring on her finger, while excitedly looking forward to her wedding day.

It wasn't long after, they were engaged, that Skeet left the dry cleaners, and got a job at Bennet & Wood as a store man, where Beryl was working.

December 20ᵗʰ, 1949

http://nla.gov.au/nla.news-article18161626

Meanwhile her brother passed his exam in Mechanical and Engineering.

HIS FATHER GOT A DEGREE

Two year old Ron Wyber of Riverstone tries on his father's mortar board after the conferring of degrees at Sydney University yesterday Ron's father Mr R Wyber received a degree of Bachelor of Mechanical & Electrical Engineering[25]

HMAS Rushcutter, RAN anti-submarine school, Rushcutters Bay, Sydney, NSW personnel undergoing training on part of the asdic (sonar) equipment, the RAN instructor is Able Seaman R A Wyber.

---

[25] *Sydney Morning Herald Thursday May 11ᵗʰ, 1950, page 24*

1950 Love and Marriage

Before they were married, Beryl and Skeet made an appointment with a Macquarie Street specialist in Sydney, to find out if she could have children. When the results came in and found out that she could, they were over the moon. After leaving the Specialist; they were crossing the road in such high spirits, and so deliriously happy, they could have hugged each other. However in those days you just didn't do that sort of thing in public.

Suddenly a car jammed on its brakes and came screeching to a stop... right in front of them. It was an old Classic, 1926 Chevrolet, with the canvas hood. The bloke leaned out the window; he had a grin on his face and said: "You don't want to let her get you that bad mate." Skeet gave him a wave and a grin. They were just so pleased with the results, both were on cloud nine. They just didn't know what they were doing, so they had to be more careful.

Chapter 19

The Wedding arrangements

From 1949 – 1950, Churches and halls were hard to get. They were extremely busy with weddings, dances, and parties. All were held on the Saturday night. People around them said: "You can't hire a Church or a hall anywhere, because they've all been booked well ahead in advance".

Not knowing what to do, Beryl wrote to her mother at the Laurel Park guest house in Burradoo. In the letter she asked her for help.

Her mother replied: "That she would make all the arrangements, and it was alright, and that she supported her decision".

The invitations were sent:

Beryl & Skeet got a week off from work, so they could get married.

The Wesley Chapel's officiating minister was the very popular Rev. Dr Frank H. Rayward. Who had become quite famous, for his charming and theatrical Wedding Services.

Mr. & Mrs. J. Burkhardt
request the pleasure of the company of

MR & MRS W. WYBER

at the
Marriage of their Daughter

Beryl
with

Reginald James Rae

at
Wesley Chapel, Castlereagh St., City

on
Saturday, 19th August, 1950

at 2.15 p.m.

and afterwards at
Cahill's, 132 Pitt Street, Sydney

R.S.V.P. 1st August   18 Cambridge Street, Elscombe

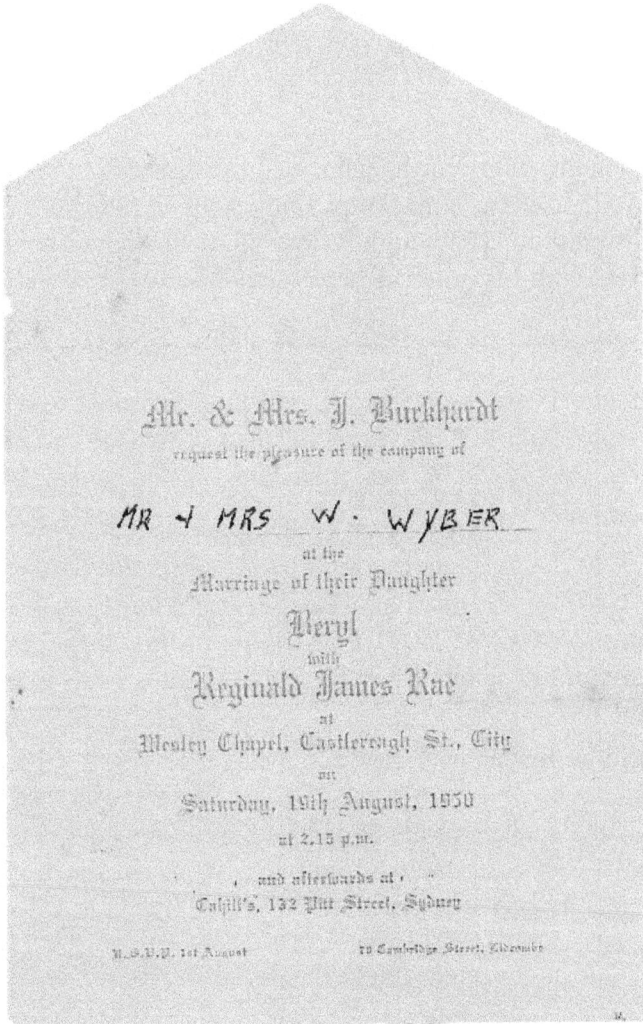

Saturday, August 19th, 1950
The Wesley Chapel, Castlereagh St, City 2:15 p.m

Skeet stood waiting at the altar, a white Carnation fixed to the lapel of the pinstripe black suit that he had borrowed from his older brother Bill.

The best man John North, who was safeguarding the wedding ring stood next to him. They both wore white shirts and a maroon dress tie. (Although beforehand, there had been some discussion with his soon to be mother-in-law Topsy, about the colour of the tie).

Topsy said: "It was an afternoon wedding; protocol was to wear a silver coloured tie". But Skeet debated these facts, wearing the maroon tie and so did the best man John North.
John Burkhardt wore the silver tie.

The air was full of anticipation as Skeet anxiously waits for the first glimpse of his bride. Beryl arriving at the Chapel is a little nervous with excitement, it's the moment she's been waiting for and dreaming of.
Beryl's auburn hair was crowned with a pearl embellish white rose bud tiara. The tiara was holding a fine mesh rose edged, chapel-length veil. Her hands held a cascading bouquet of pink and white roses. Looped around her wrist was a thin white ribbon attached to the traditional lucky white Satin horseshoe charm.

'Old wives tails depicted that 'horseshoes hung upright catch good luck, but despair will come if it tips, as all the good luck will spill out'.

Oddly enough no one had picked this up - because the horse shoe was displayed for the opposite of good luck.

Beryl's wedding gown was made by her mother, from materials of heavy satin and floral design stretch lace.

The wedding gown with long sleeves was floor length - high lace neck and had a fitted skirt. The wedding train hem was decorated with five - three inch width bows containing hundreds of small white oblong beads all hand sewn into position. The bows were set three and a half inches apart.

The flower girls; Barbara aged four her brown hair in ringlets, and Susan aged three with natural curly blonde hair, had matching headbands made of pink tulle and rosebuds. Walking hand in hand down the aisle, their transparent pink gloves held a pink ribbon tied cane basket, overflowing with pink and blue roses. They were dressed in short puffy sleeved – floor length pink satin dresses with net overlay. A golden heart necklace hung around their necks (a gift from the bride).

Following the flower girls, the maid of honour Betty King, her short cropped wavy auburn hair, was also decorated with a pink tulle and Rose flowers headband. Pale pink fingerless gloves held a small bouquet of pink roses. Betty was wearing a short puffy sleeve - pale blue, fitted floor length dress, overlayed with tulle and accessorized with mother of pearl necklace.

John Burkhardt escorted Beryl to stand next to Skeet. The Rev Frank Rayward led Beryl and Skeet into the sacred and solemn promises of the Traditional Wedding Vows, asking them to forsake all others and remain true as long as they both shall live, before God and the witnesses.

The Wedding Ring

Skeet placed the eternal symbol of love, the two toned silver and 18ct gold wedding ring with engraved edgings, on Beryl's fourth finger of her left hand.

This is where the ancients thought there was a vein that came directly from the heart, it's to remind them of their promise, and where the visible and lasting token of the covenant will never be forgotten.[26]

Pronounced man and wife, the kiss consecrates their marriage. They followed the Rev Rayward into the clerk room and with a silver pen they signed the register, the cameraman clicks the shutter. Emerging from the Chapel entrance door, Skeet is holding Beryl's hand snuggled into his, resembling a highly prized possession, while Beryl has the 'I've got my man smile' the cameraman clicks the shutter again.

---

[26] The Sydney Morning Herald, Monday 23 December 1907, page 8

Skeet and Beryl
Signing the Register

back row from left: Annie Burkhardt, John Burkhardt, Miss Betty King, John North, Eileen Rae, front row from left: Barbara Pedersen, Beryl Rae (nee Wyber) Susan Wyber, Reg Rae (Skeet) William Rae,

The Reception: was held at the Cahill's restaurant the 66 guests gathered, looking for their name place cards. Sitting upright on the tables, the cut-out name tag is between pictures of two silver bells with a white ribbon bow and small white flower, sitting against an orange circle highlighted with a yellow edging.

August is the time of the year when countless numbers of vibrant yellow daffodils grow wild in the country side. Large bunches of daffodils were arranged in crystal vases, to decorated the white linen clad tables.

Seated at the official table, is Skeet's father, Bill and mother Eileen, the Matron of honour Betty King, Skeet and Beryl, best man John North, Beryl's mother Topsy and John Burkhardt.

The Best Man: John North stood well over 6ft tall. His brushed back hair style was held firmly in place. His job was to propose the first toast and then to ensure that all subsequent speeches were both short and sweet. John was ready… with a good sense of humour to steady Skeet, who is a little stressed leading up to the bridal-Waltz.

The first Dance the Bridal Waltz

It was customary in those days as they danced the bridal waltz, for the groom to sing to the bride and Beryl had asked Skeet to sing 'The Anniversary Song' to her. Now Skeet was rather shy in front of people and as the time arrived he was getting a bit worried. But that night, with the entire crowd watching them, when he held her in his arms all he could see was her face and he could sing. He was so happy, that he sung the whole lot through for her while they danced around and around the floor and it didn't worry him one bit.

The Anniversary Song ♫
Oh, how we danced on the night we were wed
We vowed our true love, though a word wasn't said
The world was in bloom, there were stars in the skies
Except for the few that were there in your eyes

♫Dear, as I held you close in my arms
Angels were singing a hymn to your charms
Two hearts gently beating, murmuring low
"Darling, I love you so"♫

The night seemed to fade into blossoming dawn
The sun shone anew but the dance lingered on
Could we but recall that sweet moment sublime
We'd find that our love is unaltered by time

♫Darling, I love you so

The night seemed to fade into blossoming dawn
The sun shone anew but the dance lingered on
Could we but recall that sweet moment sublime
We'd find that our love is unaltered by time

Cutting of the cake

The traditional, two tiers square wedding cake was decorated with white icing, white satin bows, silver leaves and upright swirls. The top tier decorated with a miniature vase with icing flowers. The corners of the bottom tier had silver good luck horse shoes but again these good luck symbols were turned the wrong way!

Skeet's right hand rests on Beryl's while her hand guides the cutting of the cake. Smiling they hold this position, while the photographer clicks the shutter. The cake is then whisked away to be cut into portions to be handed out to leaving guests.

The bouquet thrown it was time to leave.

Beryl & Skeet cutting wedding cake

The Honeymoon

On the train, they were heading to Toronto on Lake Macquarie, just south of Newcastle for their honeymoon. They were staying, in a boarding house, not far from the station. The door and windows opened onto a front veranda. There was a miner, his wife and their kids living there permanently.

His kids were playing on the veranda. Beryl was lying on the bed and said: "Come on give me a cuddle." Skeet said: "Oh, I don't know, the kids on the veranda are making me a bit nervous." Beryl said: "They won't see us having a cuddle." Skeet said: "I don't know." he walked over and sat on the bed. Next thing the blinds rattled, then zip zip… up they go. Two little heads poked through.

Someone yelled out… "Hey! What are you kids doing… get out of there!" and the kids pull their heads back out of the window. Skeet said: "That was close wasn't it?"

After the honeymoon, they moved into a boarding house at Manly were they rented a room. They gave them a single room with two single beds. Skeet said: "that wasn't good enough for Beryl she pushed the beds together." He said: "he was a bit embarrassed of them coming in and seeing the bed changed" but it didn't bother Beryl. For about four months they were travelling back and forth to work and trying to save some money.

Chapter 20

Falls Creek

After six years Army service, Skeet's Sister Joyce and her husband Bert, left the hustle and bustle of the city. They bought a four acre property down at Falls Creek near Nowra. They put a dwelling shack on it, built of car box wood to live in. However the Council condemned it and told them to pull it down. They pleaded their case…that it was only a temporary dwelling until the house was built. The Council turned a blind eye with a warning to hurry up and get it built. Then, Joyce and Bert decided to sell their property with the shack on it, and move further up the street.

Skeet and Beryl wanted to live near Joyce. They liked the thought of a country lifestyle, and the tranquillity of the bush. So they bought Joyce and Bert's 4 acre property, located just past the Huskisson turn off. Later on, they bought another adjoining 4 acres, now they owned an eight acres property. They saved up £200, to start building their house, then moved into the shack. The oblong shaped shack was built out of two car-boxes; with a corrugated iron roof. But it wasn't long before they ran into trouble, when they found out it had been condemned by the council.

Which meant Skeet was under pressure to get the house built quickly, before the council ordered them to tear it down. They found out that the dream life-style wasn't going to be easy, especially for two people who were used to the conveniences of a city lifestyle. Bert had already dug down 6ft in the ground, for a water-well. The problem with that was… it was in the wrong place and never had any water in it at any time and never likely too, because it was dug in clay. As a result, fresh water was in short supply. Life in general was pretty tough it was a stressful time for Beryl. She struggled with the daily chores, washing clothes by hand, labouring with large items like sheets.

They started to clear the land… armed with an axe and crosscut-saw Skeet cut down the trees, and started to clear the bracken ferns with a hoe and brush cutter, followed by a burn off.

Beryl's brother in-law Bill, gave them a wind up gramophone (It was an unwanted gift, he had acquired from an officer in the Navy after he had completed some drawings for him).
For entertainment, on a clear starry night, they'd sit on a board that was covered with a blanket in front of a bonfire singing along to their favourite songs.

Sometimes Beryl would play the piano accordion, and although she never did fully master it, she could play a few tunes quite well.

Bath time was outside in a 44 gallon drum, the drum had been cut in half then propped up on bricks. A small fire lit beneath would warm the water. For privacy, Skeet had a two man tent that he used to go camping with in his single days; he erected the tent over the bath. Illuminated by kerosene light outside, they had just enough room to have a hot bath, get dressed, and then duck inside.

At first they didn't have a stove. They relied heavily on canned and preserved food and homemade damper bread. Then Skeet got a second hand fuel stove, he packed clay around it for heat retention, then built a small opened front shed to cover it. The small shed was constructed out of rough sheets of corrugated iron, and gave them shelter while they cooked their meals.

Inside the shack, the table was at one end, the bedroom at the other, with a shelf surround. It was pioneer lifestyle, with no electricity, they relied on kerosene light, and it wasn't ideal. There were lots of problems and life was hard, but they were prepared to make the sacrifices for their dream of home ownership to come true.

Old Mr Green was a builder and their neighbour; he lived across the road in a diagonal direction. They gave him £200 to build the house and Skeet helped him. Labour was intensive with no power tools, nevertheless eventually the house was built. The two bedroom fibro home had future plans for an extension of a lounge room (when they had saved up enough money) and the piers were laid in readiness for that purpose (although to this day it never did get built).

The Kitchenette had an open red brick fire place, with a mantel piece over the top which stood between two small double hung windows. The kitchen sink and cupboards on one side of the room, table and chairs in the middle.

Opposite the kitchen was the main bedroom the second bedroom was next to it. Opposite the second bedroom, was the bathroom, with exposed copper water pipes, on yellow coloured waterproof wall panels. The shower head, hung over a matching yellow coloured iron bath where water for bathing was heated with a chip heater. The back door led to an outside laundry and further down the yard, Skeet had constructed a pit toilet, basically a hole dug in the ground.

Falls Creek at that time had no services; no water, no telephone, no electricity and no mail delivery. At first they relied on an, Ice Box, later on they bought "Silent Night" kerosene fridge, light was from a kerosene wick lamp.

They decided to get a few chooks, half a dozen white leghorns. Skeet put some wire up to penned them in then decided to get a rooster for the hens, so they could have some chickens.

The hens decided they didn't like the young rooster and pecked a hole in his wing. It started to bleed so Skeet had to take the rooster out, not knowing what to do with the young rooster at night he put him in the lean to shed out the back (the cooking area near the kitchen).

Skeet used to feed him near the house. So at night just for some fun, Skeet uses to race the rooster to see who got in the door first. If the rooster won, he would take him out and try again. Eventually his wing healed and he was put back in with the hens. By this time he was a bit older so he was boss of the yard now and the hens left him alone.

Things improved even more when Skeet built a tank stand. He built it using abandoned Army block aids (tapered concrete blocks) which had been used in the war in trenches on the beach. The blocks would bring the enemy military vehicles and tanks to a halt when they run over them.

He positioned four in place and then mounted a wooden floor on top to hold a 1,000 gallon water-tank worked on gravity flow to the home.

Skeet also did all his own plumbing which saved them money and things were starting to look up.

They were settling into their new life when the doctor told Beryl that she was going to have a baby.

Home at Falls Creek "Elimatta"

The Albatross Airbase

The H.M.A.S Albatross Airbase housed and feed up to 200 workers on the base. Skeet was hired as a waiter to serve breakfast, dinner and tea. It was too far to come home between shifts, so he stayed there and didn't get home till 8 p.m. The money was good and that was going fine until the boss and his wife, who had annual leave were going away on holidays and they made Skeet head waiter, a responsibility that proved to be extremely challenging for him.

Skeet was 22 at the time, when he was confronted by old Jim. Now, old Jim was an insulting self-righteous bachelor, who did what he liked and let his dog run freely around the place. With delusions of self-grandeur, he entered the canteen, taking it upon him-self to be in charge. He was laying down the law to everyone… dictating that, that stays there, and we will wash the tea towels afterwards, you will do this and you will have extra jobs to do!

All day he continued to dictate that no one was going home until everything was done.

Poor Skeet; was over powered by old Jim. So he looked to Bert (who was working around the place doing maintenance as a groundsman) to asked him for some advice on how to handle the situation.

Bert, offering some friendly advice started talking to the other two waiters and suggested… The only way of beating old Jim was… You start on time and you finish on time, and if you can't get it all done, then old Jim will just have to do it himself.
Bert said:

> 'And if Old Jim doesn't like it, then there was
> going to be a strike! and you're quite within your
> rights to go on strike.'

The waiters listen to Bert and agreed with him. Skeet was getting a bit worried about it and said: "Look you can't do that," but they'd made up their minds.
Shaking his head Skeet said: "Alright then", and he went along with it but he didn't like it. Well… that riled old Jim right up as Skeet was setting the tables and taking food orders from the workers… Old Jim was following him around brow beating him, about what was going on.

Finally fed up with Old Jim! Skeet faced him and said: "Look I am sorry, but I have to go along with them. We are going to work for the normal two hours." (Usually, we would have started a bit earlier, so we could take the orders and have the

164

meals cooked, and ready to serve the men when they walked in the door.)

Well! Old Jim put on an act; he was blaming Skeet for everything. Skeet was fuming and said: "Just a minute, I am not going to take this'. Skeet started too shaped up to him saying: "Look here! We will have it out right here and now", and gave it to him right in front of all the men. Out gunned, Old Jim backed down, he wasn't about to fight him, and walked straight out the door. Skeet thought he had him. After the boss came back from holidays, next thing Skeet knew he was sacked.

June 9, 1951. First child

It was during this turbulent time, when Skeet was working as head waiter. That the Doctor advised Beryl, she needed to have a caesarean delivery due to some complications, and giving her a warning as with any other major surgery or surgical procedure risks were involved.

Beryl was booked into the Royal North Shore Hospital on Thursday June 7th in preparation for the birth of their child. Around this time it was close to her sister birthday 9th June so she choose to have her baby then.

The day she had been preparing for arrived, iron levels checked, drip inserted, catheter, the anaesthesia administered, blood pressure and heart rates monitored. They wheeled her into the operating theatre. Doctor Moon was waiting, he made his first incision with the second incision he entered the womb, breaking the nourishing amniotic sac. The surgeon worked quickly in a pulling and twisting motion until he had successfully delivered a baby girl. Cleaned and tested Apgar, (Appearance, Pulse, Grimace, Activity, and Respiration), Beryl smiled hearing her baby cry.

165

The surgeon working quickly to stitch and stapled there was considerable loss of blood, so a transfusion was needed before they wheeled her back to recovery.

At this time… Skeet was still working at the Works Camp as head waiter and couldn't get away to be with Beryl. He was waiting there for a phone call. That's when they said:

> "Is there something wrong with you? You're expecting a kid, waiting for the phone to ring? You're supposed to be walking up and down the corridor smoking cigarettes"

But all day he was thinking of her… and wondering what was happening and how she was going. At some time he got the message it's a girl and they are OK. But still he couldn't go straight away because that would have left others in a spot for work.

When Beryl was released from hospital she went to stay with her sister Dot at 70 Cambridge Street, Lidcombe until she was strong enough to go back home.
Lorraine had just been bathed and dressed in a pretty short sleeve dress.
The sun radiating from the window, gleams on a gold 9ct baby bracelet, with a padlock heart on Lorraine's wrist, the name plate yet to be engraved is florally decorated.

Dot grabs the camera. Beryl, kneeling on the floor props Lorraine up on the bunny rug and smiles devotedly.

Heaven's Special Mum

Lorraine & Beryl Rae

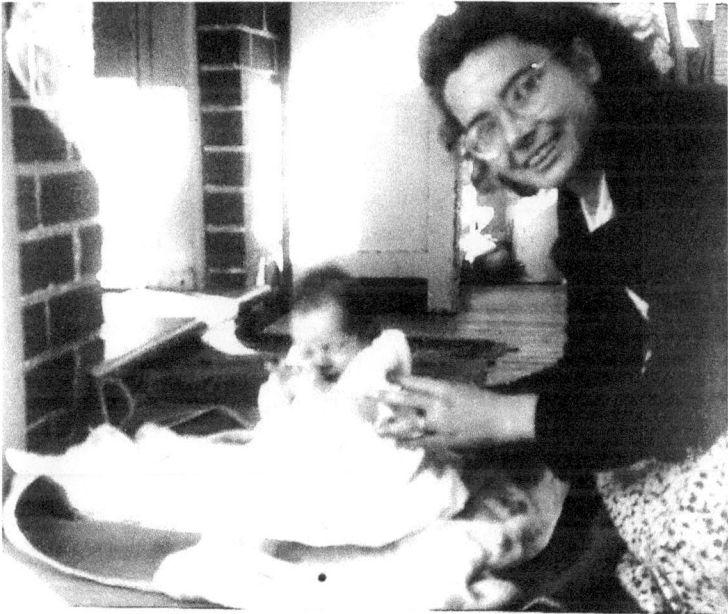

Chapter 21

Partnership

The Responsibility of a new baby weighed heavily on Skeet, because he had no job and no money, they were doing it tough. Beryl was overjoyed with her new baby, but at the same time was a little disappointed, because her mother wasn't happy about it.

In 1951 Bert Guest was 34, has straight dark brown hair, in a brush back style, eyes grey, and stood 5ft 6 tall. Unfortunately while he was serving in the Australian Army in Darwin in March 1945, he had suffered injuries of a traumatic amputation of his right hand, when he slipped while adjusting the guide of a working circular saw on the bench and he was discharged in Dec 1945.

The Army compensated him with a War Pension and financially that made life a little easier for both of them. Joyce was 28 then.

Nevertheless... it made life difficult when he had to drive a car, because he needed it for hand signals. To solve the problem he melted celluloid over a wire, which was fashioned into the shape of a hand then painted it with a bit of flesh coloured paint. Attaching it to the stump of his right arm, he could then give hand signals while driving the car.

168

Skeet was broke after losing his job at the Works Camp. There wasn't much work around at the time, so he and Bert decided to go into partnership cutting Cordwood for the brickworks.

This work involved cutting up logs into 6 feet lengths, then stacking them for the pick-up truck. The local Brick Works used them to stoke the fire of the Kiln. Bert wasn't as hungry for the money as Skeet and the partnership soon split up.

October 1951, Bob and his family were going to live in England for a couple of years, due to an offer of a government job. Bob, Nancyé's family, neighbours and friends came to wish them Bon-voyage before they sailed away.

A professional photographer on board the ship took a photo in remembrance of the day. From left to right: Barbara is standing alongside her parents Bill and Dot Pedersen, next Robyn Wyber is standing in front of her mother Flora.

Sitting down, Beryl is holding four months old Lorraine fascinated by her cousin's blonde ringlets, keeps reaching out to grab a handful of her hair. Robyn with a protective hand covers her hair while consoled by her grandmother (Topsy) with a loving arm around her; looking stern John Burkhardt is standing behind them.

Ron is standing next to his Nan his sister Susan embraced by her mother Nancy'e. Bob is standing at the back with Nancyé sister–in-law and her brother along with two small children. Before they leave Nancyé gives Beryl, her own much treasured and beautiful Old English Pram with a detachable hood, the one she had used for her babies, saying that Beryl could use it for Lorraine.

Bob didn't know it then, but it was the last time, he would see his sister, and the last photo taken of Beryl.

Left back row: Dot & Pete Pedersen, Flora Wyber, John Burkhart,- - - Raymond Vaughan, -Bob Wyber.

Front row: Barbara Pedersen, Robyn Wyber, Beryl Rae holding Lorraine, Robyn Pedersen, Topsy Burkhardt, Ron Wyber, Mary Vaughan, Susan Wyber, Nancye Wyber, -, -

Chapter 22

The Good Times

Skeet was in between jobs when he started working with his neighbour Mr Green. He was assisting him building houses and doing a bit of plumbing. Then he applied for and got a job working at Button's Dry Cleaners in Nowra, owned by Glass & Sayer.

He had been working there for quite some time doing spotting and cleaning.

Every day rain, hail or shine Skeet would ride his push-bike back and forth to work it was roughly a 12 mile trip all up. Once a week Beryl would come into town with Lorraine, to do the weekly shopping and have lunch with him. While Skeet was at work, Lorraine, Beryl and Joyce spent most days together. Beryl was five years younger than her sister-in-law Joyce; however their birthdays on 26th and 27th October were only a day apart.

Joyce was slim built, and stood about 5ft 5". Her well-groomed wavy brunette hair was cut medium length. Her dark eyes sparkled with youthful exuberance, she was quick witted and fun loving, and had an infectious smile. She loved the sun and had an olive skin to accommodate it.

Being the eldest girl in the family, Joyce had a strong protective and caring nature. As they were growing up, she took it upon her-self to protect her younger siblings, which she had more than once... standing up to the sisters of the Catholic School, to defend her little brother Skeeter.

Beryl and Joyce were good friends and because Beryl's back wasn't strong, every day Joyce would bathe Lorraine for her. Around this time Skeet and Beryl were also enjoying a good social life with neighbours Win and Ron Henderson, they had two little girls. On alternate Saturday night's they would go to each other's house for a game of cards. Card night was always a light hearted one with a bit of good natured cheating and jokes, along with tea and cake.

Occasionally, Beryl and Skeet would catch the bus into Nowra to attend the 1930's style Roxy Movie Theatre, located in Berry Street.

When the picture had ended they caught the bus home. On the way home, everyone in the bus would join in a sing song.

In those days, the bus driver had no designated stops, he would pull over whenever someone wanted him too. It was around this time that the bush-fires came through.

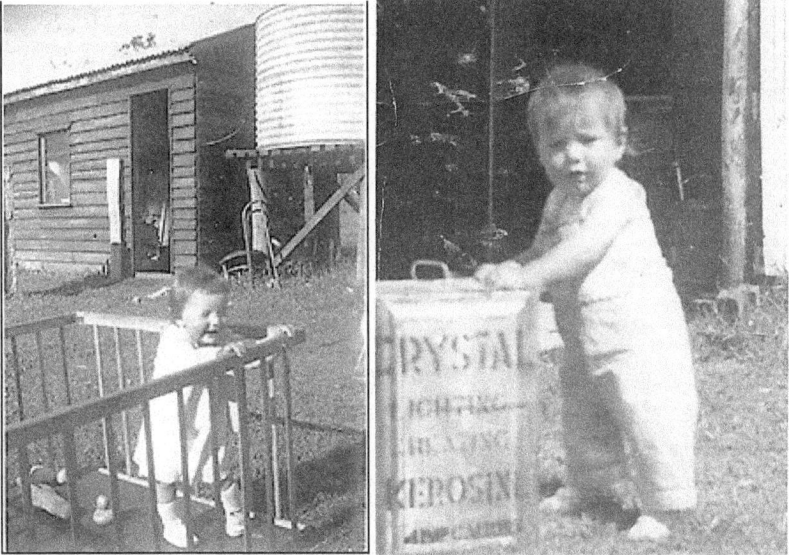

Lorraine 1952

'Black Friday'

1952 was one hell of a year! one that Skeet will remember for the rest of his life, and wishes he could forget. It was the end of January, after a prolonged dry spell. The weather forecast was for a hot and sultry day with considerable cloudiness in most parts of the State.

Three of the States were hit by a heat wave New South Wales, Victoria and South Australia, with temperatures in Sydney ranging from 71 F degrees (22 C) at 5:15 am to 82.5 F degrees (28 C) at 12.20 pm. In Victoria the temperature in Melbourne soared to 109.7 F degrees (43 C) at 4pm.

This was the highest reading since January 13th 1939.

The bush fires blazed out of control in the wild country of the State Forests creating hell on earth, spreading over a wide area.

A phone call came through to 'Buttons Dry Cleaners. The Boss told Skeet to get home because the bush fires were raging down there.

So he had to get on his push-bike and ride home.

He was more than halfway, when he reached the turn off at the Albatross Naval Base Aerodrome. Plumes of grey smoke towered into the sky and he still had three miles to go. The smoke was so thick, that he couldn't see the road ahead, but he had to get home. Knowing the road was straight he took a deep breath and peddled like blazes.

Unable to hold his breath any longer, he inhaled the smoke... Coming out the other side of the thick smoke he was coughing and spluttering.

It took him about 30 seconds before he could stop coughing and was alright again. Taking a few deep breaths, he filled his lungs with fresh air. After a while he was OK so he pressed on.

The wind driven fire, was moving quickly now, burning the layers of rotting dead leaves, stringy bark and undergrowth then, exploding up the thickets of gum trees, throwing flaming embers ahead of it creating a firestorm!

When Skeet arrived home, the place was still standing but the threat was close. Waiting nervously for Skeet, out the front of the house Beryl was looking fearful of what was happening she was dressed in her house frock. Lorraine wearing a singlet and nappy was being held by Joyce. They were relieved to see him.

Although you couldn't see the flames, the radiation from the heat was intense. Skeet could feel his face drying out and

174

starting to burn. He could see that it was too late for back burning.

There were people living behind them, and if he started to back burn to save his place they would be trapped and he couldn't take the risk. By this time the house was in trouble, there was nothing he could do to stop the flames.

The unfinished home, had open eves that drew the fire into the home. Fuelled by the exploding kerosene fridge, the intensity was increased. Next thing the windows shattered.

Hopelessly, Skeet stood there watching knowing there was nothing he could do. So he did what he could to save the animals. He went around the back to let the chooks out. The flames were too close to the gate of the chicken run, so to give them a chance, he pulled the chicken wire off the side of the coop but that's all he could do.

His clothes offered little protection from the radiant heat, and his skin was starting to burn, so he took off.

The Fire raged for three days and two nights. The glare from forest fires turned the night sky red.

The volunteering men struggled with the fires. Armed only with an old bush rake they rake up the leaves burn them, and then left quickly because of the intensity of the heat radiating from them. When the flames died down they would belt it out with a large flap, forming a pathway between them and the fires. Each night the men fought the fires building fire breaks. They managed to save a lot of the houses. When they were tired they would just jump into a drum of cold water, and it woke them up and kept them going.

The RSL Club came around with a keg of warm beer to drink, and asked Skeet if he wanted some. He said: "no thanks I would go to sleep". The Salvation Army came around with a large drum full of tea, so Skeet had the tea to give him a pick up. The beer would have made him sleepy, although it wouldn't take much for him to go to sleep.

One of the men had rubber gumboots on and was wearing shorts, when a spark went down his gumboot. Suddenly he threw down his rake he was yelling out while trying to put the spark out when he stamped his foot down on an upturned rake. The rake went right through his gumboot up into his foot. He managed to get it out, although he was cursing a bit.

The men being so tired all they could do was laugh for being so stupid, but another time you would have been more sympathetic. Skeet along with the other men, were weary. Indifferently, they asked him to show them again, how he had done it.

Skeet found a place to rest on the side of the road. He lay down, the rocks felt like an innerspring mattress. Everyone was exhausted, he was about to drop off into a deep sleep… when the man next to him nudged him. He said: "See that new bloke over the other side of the road with his brush". He had noticed his trousers were on fire, and you could see it was smouldering at the back.

Skeet said: "Tell him," He said: "No, you tell him." Skeet looked up utterly exhausted, he didn't have a yell in him, and said: "Bugger it, he'll find out soon enough, then stuck their heads down. Well it passed his boots then he started to feel the heat. He turned around and had figured it out. Next thing… he was yelling and jumping up and down, they all had a bit of a chuckle.

176

In the aftermath of the fires that swept through Falls Creek, seven homes and a builder's worker camp were lost, and they had lost their home.

A Gruesome Scene
Their dream had turned into a nightmare

Skeet and Beryl returned home… to find a tortured smouldering landscape. Their dream had turned into a nightmare, horrified they stood sadly amidst the ruins. The hungry, monstrous fire had sucked the life out of their home, leaving them with only charred remnants of timber frames and twisted metal roofing.

The only thing left standing was the brick chimney. Like a tombstone in remembrance of what could have been.

With taut faces and a heavy brow… they began to pick through the after effects of the devastation.

The beautiful old English pram...gone, the furniture and all their wedding gifts... gone, and 'The Badge of Fortitude,' like the symbol of her courage was melted somewhere among the ruins, Beryl broke down and cried.

Skeet, while thoughtful of all the work and sacrifices they'd made, now seemingly for nothing… tried to comfort Beryl.

He found the Crystal decanter set, a wedding gift from his brother John, melted down the brick wall of the fire-place.

His gun barrel lay warped across the remains of a charred table. The chooks, unable to escape the intense radiant heat, had all perished, and laid next to each other all in a row.

When they moved the front door mat surprisingly they found the grass was still green underneath. Then he remembered... that just two days earlier, he'd paid insurance on the home. However, when he went in to see them to make a claim, they argued the point saying they hadn't processed it yet, and were reluctant to pay-up. Eventfully they did pay.

One farmer who came down said to them, that there was room up at his place, and that his mother had said to let them know. She had a sewing machine and she would help them to sew dresses. They thanked them very much, and said: "They already had an offer to rent a garage cheaply up the street."

The garage was opposite Joyce and Bert's place. It was lined, and had a kitchen with a stove, a bedroom, a fire place and laundry outside.

It was amazing! People came from everywhere to help them. The Apex Club took up collections of money, to help rebuild their place. The McGuire family came down from Tomerong a big family of them. They were in the timber business, and cut the timber on their land using axes and crosscut saws with two long teeth for cutting and a smaller tooth to rake the sawdust out of the cut.

They had a team of twelve to fourteen bullocks' driven by teamsters to drag the log to the jinkers. The jinkers, had two very large wagon-type wheels six or seven feet high.
The wheels straddled the log and it was loaded on by a jack attached to a crank, then secured with chains and taken to the

Mill. The Mill cut them and gave Skeet what they needed to rebuild. The bullocks' then hauled it back again all for nothing. The Mill did alright out of it as well; they kept what they didn't need.

Re – Building

Family, friends and others came to lend a helping hand, and they were rebuilding the place back up.

Skeets brother Jack gave him money to pay for insurance on the new home. Beryl's brother Bob and his wife Nancýe in England also wanted to help sent money.

The Brickworks, donated the bricks they ordered. However when they delivered the timber from the mill, it had been raining. Because they couldn't get onto the block they off loaded it on the side of the highway. Skeet couldn't leave it there, because it was too easy for someone to take it, and someone could have had an accident, by running into it in the dark.

Then they would have been in all sorts of trouble. So he put on a rain coat, and went out, to shift it by himself onto the block. Beryl arrived not long after wanting to help.

 He said: "Hey" What you are doing down here… its hard work". He was worried about her, because of her back. She looked up… with a little hurt look, and said: "I just wanted to help."
Skeet couldn't knock her back and said:

> "Alright love, you get one end of the timber and
> I'll get the other, and we will carry it one piece at
> a time."

It was slow going because he stopped for a few rests, out of concern for Beryl. It was all about being together and helping each other out, the timber was eventually moved. The plumber in town was selling them iron for the roof. Another plumber, who was a relative of Beryl's, came down and said: "That's unbranded Iron." Skeet said: "It looks alright." The plumber said: "It's good stuff but it's not 100%".

Skeet rang them up and went in to see them. So they were found out they had done their sheets, and lost the job. Then Beryl's uncle supplied them with the 100% iron for the roof. They gave him their order number, because he took it off another job. He could re-order and replace the iron back for his job. So it ended up they had all this nice iron to make a shed, which made everyone pretty envious.

They had hoped to have the place finished by eight hour week end (6th October).

Albatross Naval Base

Skeet started working a couple of days a week, at the Albatross Naval Base, building the Engine Test Stands, for the Airplanes.

The stands supported the turboprop engines, during performance testing. .

The trouble was… it got so bitterly cold up there, you had to have a fire to warm your hands up just to pick up a nail and then knock that in, then warm your hands again to pick up the next nail and knock it in. To sign anything you had to hold the pen with two hands, to stop it from shaking.

Skeet later traded that job for a warmer place in a Dry Cleaning job with Hawkins on the Albatross Base.

A dog named Mike

Beryl got a dog. She called him Mike; nobody knew where it came from. It was a non-descript looking thing, a large dog standing about a metre or so high coloured brown & black with big floppy ears and big feet. Skeet said:

> "It was the most useless guard-dog he'd ever come across. If a burglar came round the place, it would probable lick him to death and show them were all the good stuff was (not that they had any good stuff at that stage)."

Mike liked to go out with the chickens that were running about in the back yard.

Mike loved those chickens. He used to put its paw on them, and lick them and wash them clean, until they were gasping for breath. Skeet then had to revive them by picking them up and putting them near the fuel stove, to warm them up. When they were dried off, they were returned to the back yard and off they'd go running around and chirping again.

Chapter 23

Sold shares

Topsy and John sold their shares in Laurel Park. Now with money in the bank and her children raised and married. They felt they deserved a holiday, and it was going to be a good one. John wanted to take Topsy to Switzerland, to show her where he grew up, and to meet his family and friends.

Topsy's Trip Book

Tuesday 29 April 1952: Woolloomooloo in Sydney departed from wharf 8 on-board the 20,000 ton R. M. S. Orontes Orient Line Ship. They stood on deck until they had passed through 'The Heads' then went down to their cabin, the number on the door 119-20.

After resting for a while they unpacked. By now the ship was well out to sea. It was raining heavily, the weather became rough. That night Topsy was unwell, unable to eat dinner she went to bed around 8 p.m.

The next day... Topsy got up for breakfast but didn't retain it for long and had to be escorted back to her cabin, where she stayed for the rest of the day.

Thursday 1 May 1952: around 8 a.m. arriving at Port Melbourne, they travelled into the City going to places of interest, Art Gallery, Museum, Parliament House, St Pauls Cathedral, St Patricks Cathedral then had lunch at "Tea Pot Inn." and did a little sightseeing for a couple of days.

s.s. "ORONTES"
May 14th, 1952

This is to certify that

Anne Buckland

crossed the " Line " at Longitude

85 Degrees, 15 Minutes East on

this day and is duly admitted

to the Ancient Order of the Deep—

Davy Jones
HIS MAJESTY'S SCRIBE

Neptunus Rex
RULER OF THE RAGING MAIN

Saturday 3 May1952: It was raining heavily as they made their way back to the ship, they set-sail at noon.

Sunday 4 May 1952: it's a beautiful day with clear blue skies and the ocean was a deep blue, just perfect. Set watches back 30 minutes. 5:30p.m. berthed at Adelaide, there was a great crowd on the wharf to welcome the boat.
Around 6:30p.m. Catching the train into Adelaide was 14 miles journey from the Harbour. After touring the City they left at midnight, returning to the ship.

Friday 9 May 1952: On deck it was quite hot in the sun, spent the morning reading and rested after lunch, in preparation for dinner and The Gala Dance night.

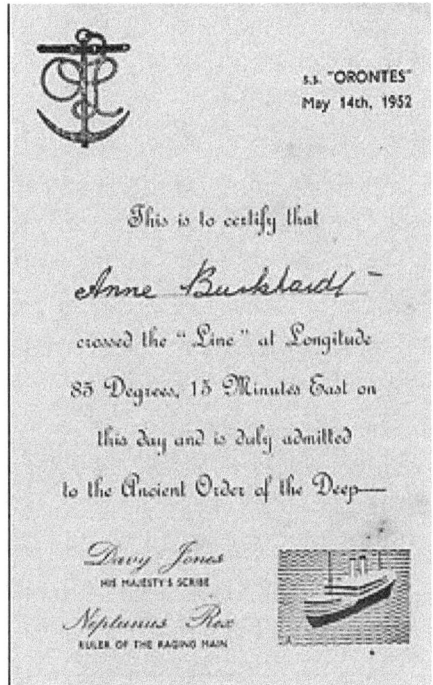

Sunday 11 May 1952: The heat was terrific - too hot to sleep in cabins, issued with beds to sleep on deck. Not feeling well - Topsy entered sick bay.

Wednesday 14 May 1952: Signed name on a light blue certificate card, which stated Annie Burkhardt crossed the Line at Longitude 85 Degrees, 15 minutes east, and is duly admitted to the Ancient Order of the Deep Davy Jones.

Thursday 15 May 1952: Arrived at Colombo, still in sick bay, not allowed to go ashore.

Monday 19 May 1952: Out of sick bay today, the heat was still terrific.

Tuesday 20 May 1952: Arrived at Aden 8 p.m. Goats roaming the streets, beggars followed them, natives asking them to buy souvenirs, natives sleeping on pavements. Back to the boat - set sail, passed some very interesting groups of Islands.

Wednesday 21 May 1952: A race meeting was held on D-deck which was also a beer garden - sing songs, funny face, knobbly knee and bathing beauty competition. In the evenings dances on E-Deck. A Fancy dress Ball on D-Deck with marvellous buffet suppers beautifully laid out.

Thursday 29 May 1952: Arrived at the Port of France, Marseilles, 6 a.m. had breakfast; 8 a.m. checked through customs around 9 a.m. caught a bus into Marseilles, later-on caught the train that left at midnight for Genève. 'Cooks Tours' had booked them into 'The Le Grand Hotel.'

There was plenty of time to go sightseeing; everything was expensive in this town a fish lunch cost £3, so they decided on a bread roll with a Frankfurt, and then sat in the Park to eat it.

While there they watched a communist demonstration. Police were patrolling the streets on push bikes, in batches of thirty long and two deep, they searched houses for communist activity. It was also a religious day; girls dressed in long white frocks, boys with white ribbons tied on their arms above the elbow, wearing white gloves.

It was near midnight, when they arrived at the Marseilles Railway station. It had a magnificent entrance, but the train was in very poor condition, worse than Sydney trains and it was running about 20 minutes late.

Friday 30 May 1952: Around 9 a.m. arrived at Genève, went through customs. The French checked their passports, and then a few yards further on, the Swiss also checked their passports this is the border.

Had two hours to wait for a train to Alten, so visited the markets bought 2½ lbs of cherries for one shilling and 10 oranges for one shilling, commented that they were very cheap. Waiting at the Railway Station, before boarding the train had coffee and buns at the Stations Café. On the train trip the scenery was gorgeous, as every few yards there was something different to look at.

Arrived at Alten 3 p.m. it was located near the German border; John's twin sisters Marie and Moll, were at the station to meet them, and gave them a great welcome with big warm hugs. John's family home was situated on the river, it was a lovely sight. Meet, John's eldest sister Nellie, they stayed over there for over two months and meet quite a few of John's old girl friends. He was quite enjoying himself and Tospy felt like a prized exhibit.

Saturday it was daylight until 9 p.m. they walked around the village and visited the markets in the streets here they sold pigs, cows, fruit and veggies there were all sorts of stalls and it was very busy because everyone goes to the market in the afternoon. Went back to the home and had a sleep, John and Nellie took flowers to the Cemetery.

After tea another of John's friends visited them, he had spent five years in Australia so again Topsy was able to join in the conversations. Most evenings were spent talking (in German) while Topsy listen and tried to look intelligent. Saturday night 8 p.m. all the Church bells started ringing in Sunday, they had rung for 15 minutes all different chimes. The next day at 8 a.m. all church bells rang again, to let you know it is Sunday.

Travelling extensively through Switzerland, they caught a bus to a village named Erlenbach, viewing beautiful scenery along the way. On the farms all hands were out in the fields harvesting the crops.

Leaving the bus, they visited a very old church and grave yard. Most of the houses in Erlenbach are five to six hundred years old. Next, they visited another friend of the family at a very old farm house for afternoon tea, consisting of a platter of four different sausages, slice of ham, slice of pork, great hunks of bread all washed down with red and white wine.

Then they walked for 1 hour to another village Schonenwerd, and visited another home. There were 80 white leghorn hens and quite a number of black rabbits in pens. The old lady who looked after the animals as well as the garden was 80-years-old. Didn't stay long, still had a couple of calls to make.

Finally, ended up at a school girl friend of John's, had another feed of fish, wine, biscuits then coffee and cherry snaps. Her 82-year-old mother and 84-year-old father were out gardening, it was a beautiful garden. Topsy was amazed how these old people still work in this country. Left there 7 p.m. and caught the train back home to Alten.

Socializing all day and partying late into the evening with John's family and friends were getting too much for Topsy leaving her exhausted and she let John go on his own to reunions with his old mates, while she lazed in bed and wrote twelve cards to Australia, then did some laundry.

Friday 15 July 1952: A three hour train ride took John, Nelly, Alice & Topsy right across Switzerland viewing snow-capped mountains and lakes, to the town of Lugarno. Arrived at 12:30 p.m. the village was decorated with flags and gardens it was carnival time. Discovering quite a few souvenir shops, Topsy bought a table cloth for both Dot and Beryl.

Saturday 2 August 1952: It was time to leave, there was quite a crowd come to see them off. They hugged and made promises to keep in touch and you will have to come and visit, and take care of yourself.
It was with a heavy heart they left Alten on the 9 p.m. train.

Around 1:00 a.m. Arrived at Basle; it was 11:00 a.m. the next day when they arrived at Boulogne-Sur-mer in France stayed overnight, before purchasing a ticket for the boat train.

Sunday 3 August 1952: The boat left Paris, around noon. It was a 1½ hour trip across the English Channel and was extremely rough. It didn't agree with Topsy. Arriving at Folkestone Harbour Railway Station they boarded 'The Golden Arrow' steam train, the carriages were double glazed and air conditioned with prestige service, including the Trianon Bar, there Destination: Victoria Station, London.

Arriving around 4:30 p.m. they walked through Hyde Park to Paddington Station to change trains, caught the 5:30 p.m. train, travelling South West for their final destination in Bristol to see Bob and Nancy'e. It was raining heavily when they arrived around 8:30 p.m. They'd been travelling now for approximately twenty three and a half hours.

Her son Bob was there to meet them at the station, they took a taxi up to Belvoir Road where the family rented a fashionable three story unite. Topsy said: she was some-what impressed with Bristol.

Wednesday 13 August 1952: Visit to the Zoo; it was the world's oldest, opened in 1836. At the Zoo Ron and Sue rode on a camel and were quite disappointed at not being able to have a ride on Rosie the Elephant. So they gave Rosie pennies, Rosie gave them to her keeper. Then Nan and Topsy took time out to go shopping.

Friday 15 August 1952: Topsy wanted to catch up with her late husband William's relatives, they lived further north in Newcastle-on-Tyne. Left Bristol early around 5:15 a.m. arrived at Westland's Road, visited (William's sister) Chrissy and her husband Thomas Sanderson with their two children Eric and Kenneth.

Living close by were other family members, arranged to have tea with (William's other sister), Agnes and her husband Russel, children Peter and Stella. Then visited Doris, Norm Wallace and Ethel Wyber, around 10 p.m. arrived back at Chrissy's to see (William's brother) Adam and his second wife Ina, spent a few hours with them, before heading back to the "Corner House Hotel," around midnight.

The next day: there were sad farewells and promises to write, before it was time to go. They were about an hour into the return trip home to Bristol, before Nancy'e realized she had left her purse behind, so they had to turn around and go back to get it.

Thursday 4 September 1952 Time to leave Bob, Nancye, Susan and Ron, after prolonged farewell hugs and kisses, said goodbye. Then they caught the 6 p.m. train to London, caught a taxi-ride into the heart of the city and stayed overnight at 'The Strand Palace Hotel' opposite Trafalgar Square before the return trip home.

Bob Nancye, Susan & Ron
Trafalgar Square

August 31st, 1952, the Blue Air Mail Letter

Meanwhile back in Australia Beryl hadn't been feeling very well that morning. Maybe she'd been overdoing it, what with the ongoing stresses and the troubles of rebuilding, along with a active young child. Her mother had been gone now for over four months and Beryl had been missing her. Seated at the kitchen table, Beryl wrote her a letter.

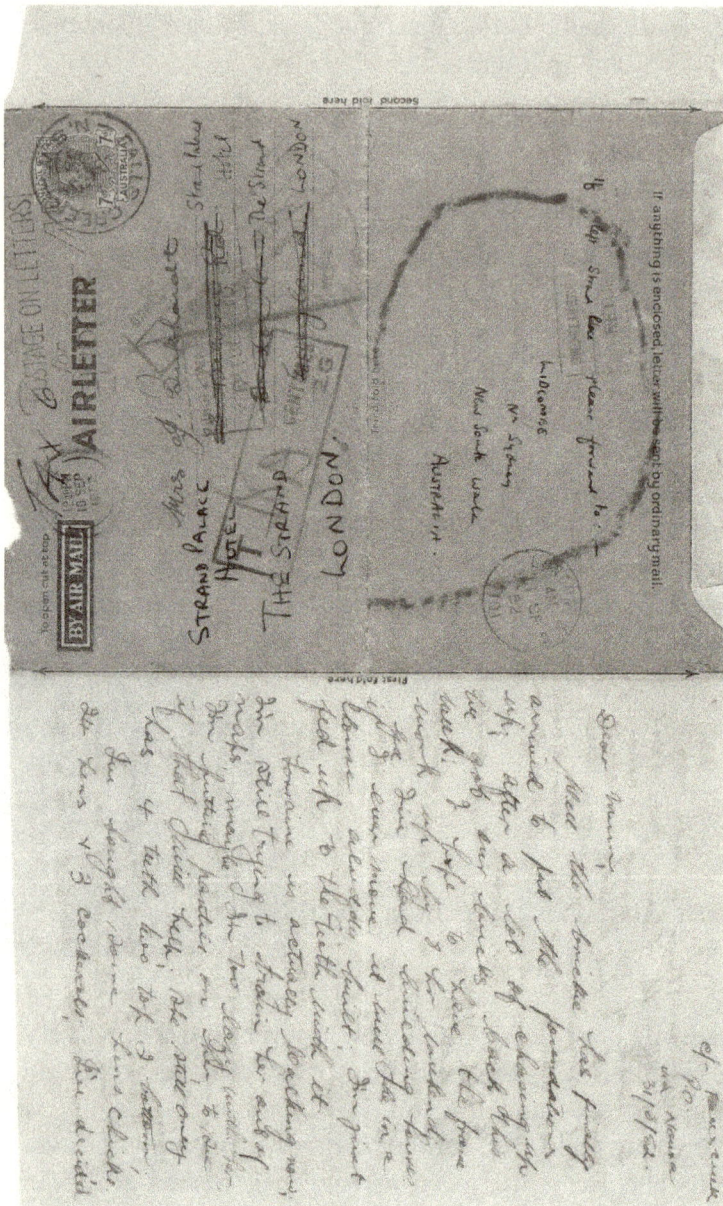

31/8/52

Dear Mum,

Well the brickie has finally arrived to put the foundations up. After a lot of chasing up we got our bricks back this week. I hope to have the frame work up by 8 hour weekend. Gad I've had building houses if I ever move it will be in a house already built, I'm just fed up to the teeth with it.

Lorraine is actually walking now, I'm still trying to train her out of naps, maybe I'm too lazy with her. I'm putting panties on her to see if that will help; she still only has 4 teeth two top 2 bottom;

I've bought some hens chicks 24 hens & 3 cockerels, I've decided to get something to take my mind off the house poor skeet he's sick of me trying to chase people up, but I told him, we won't get anywhere by sitting down we can't start the orchard until we move down & put a fence up from the cattle;

I told you we had another dog didn't I?

There was a terrible accident the other day just near our burnt block 2 men were burnt to death they believe they were unconscious anyway I sincerely hope they were, no one could do anything for them, only young men too.

Another accident happened yesterday the other side of our block a motor cycle crashed into a cow the cow had to be shot, & one of the boy's is critically injured .

It must be jonahed down there perhaps I should call it that instead of 'Elimatta'

How's the Wyber family? When will they be returning? & when will you? Glad you like England

What are, Chrissy Wyber's family like?

Well I must away to get Lorraine's dinner so cheerio

Love from Bev & Skeet

Love to the Wyber's   xxx from Lorraine

192

The blue Air-mail letter, addressed to: Mrs J Burkhardt 38 Belvoir Road, Bristol England: posted and stamped at Falls Creek P.O: on Wednesday 3 September 1952. Arrived in Bristol P.O 12:30 p.m. Wednesday 10 September 1952. Delivered to Bob & Nancy'e mail box, Thursday 11 September, the day her mother and John had left to come home on the Cruise Ship.

Topsy and John arriving at St Pancras Station, caught the 10:45 a.m. train destined for Port of Tilbury Dock, they boarded the 22,000 ton Cruise Ship, S.S. Strathnaver P&O Line, and settled in for the 35 days return trip home.

Wednesday 16 October 1952: With memories of the holiday's filling their head and loaded with souvenirs gifts of scarfs, ornamental brass shoes, Ivory paper knife, ornamental peacock, shirts, cigarette holders, broaches, Jewel box, necklaces, bracelets, ink stand, Orontes souvenir ash trays and spoons for the family, they were now anxious to be home.

Friday, around 8am: They cruised through Sydney Heads, they were happy to be home in Aussie. It was around 11am before they passed through Customs. Anxiously waiting for them was Topsy's daughter, Dot, six year old Barbara and four year old Robyn. Topsy and John stayed with Dot for a couple of weeks, before Dot drove them to see William, Flora and Robyn Wyber, and to pick up their green Hillman Minx, before driving home to Wollongong.

The Air-Mail letter

The blue Air-mail Letter: Unable to find its owner in Bristol was now stamped undelivered, re-addressed then posted to the Strand Palace Hotel. Unable to find Tospy, was then incorrectly re-addressed, to Lidcombe Nth Sydney, N S W. Australia, and stamped: 'Return to Sender'.

Chapter 24

Ten Days before Christmas

MOnday, 15 December, 1952. The morning sun rose early in the eastern sky, filtering its heated rays through the open windowpane. Peering outside the clear blue sky meant it was going to be another warm one. Beryl was happily three months pregnant with their second child and showing a baby bump.

The Christmas cards had all been posted, written with messages of love and good wishers to their families and friends. Skeet had cut a small pine tree from the surrounding bushlands; it was enhanced with ornaments and Christmas sparkles and stood in readiness for the gifts.

In the township of Nowra, Skeet had lay-byed his wife a rocking chair. He had almost finished paying for it and had planned to bring it home at the end of the week gift wrapped in Christmas paper.

That Monday was like any other day of the week, in the small country settlement of Falls Creek, quiet and uneventful. However; Skeet woke that morning feeling a bit uneasy... yet didn't understand why. It was because of these feelings, that he asked Beryl not to come down to the house with his lunch that day, he made her promise to stay there and he would come home for lunch, then they would walk down together.

And she did promise not to come.

And that's when it happened!

Yeah...

After an early breakfast Skeet set off to start work on re-building their home. It was sometime later that morning when Beryl pushing Lorraine in the stroller left the converted garage they were renting, walked across The Princes Highway to arrive at Joyce's place just on the other side of the road.

As usual Joyce bathed Lorraine, while they chuckle and chatted about this and that and because it was nearly Christmas, Joyce's son's Beau eight and Ricky nearly seven were at home because of the school holidays.. Around 10:00 a.m. Joyce put the kettle-on and called out to the boys to come inside for morning tea.

It was after midday and Skeet hadn't arrived yet, not wanting to wait any longer Beryl decided that she was going down to the house to see Skeet.
Lorraine now clean and freshly dressed was put in the stroller; everyone headed out the door. Joyce pushed the stroller as they walked the 100 yards along the gum tree lined dirt and pebble driveway, before reaching the gateway of the property.

Handing the stroller over to Beryl, Joyce smiled and waved goodbye to Lorraine and Beryl saying: 'See you tomorrow' and they both waved back. Then seeing her neighbour across the road, Joyce and the boys crossed the highway for a chat.

196

The house Skeet and Beryl were building was located about half a mile down the Hwy. Turning left in a northerly direction, Beryl started pushing the stroller along the straight and narrow two lane road.

The Princes Highway had a slight downward run from the South to the North. Deep open gutters run parallel alongside the road, beyond that were fences and open bushland. With no foot path, there was no alternative but to walk along the edge of the road presenting a dangerous journey for an unwary pedestrian.

Hugged by the warm breeze they walked under the midday sun, they watched native birds in flight, listened to the noisy cicadas sing their songs. As each step was taken toward the house to see Skeet, the wheels of the stroller rattled and rolled along the edge of the lumpy bumpy surface of the black bitumen road. The once flourishing wild bush flowers she used to pick were gone now. The aftermath of the fire had left behind a tortured landscape, harsh and eerie covered in powdery grey ash with protruding black stumps.

They had been walking for about thirteen minutes into the fifteen minute journey. Being around lunch time there wasn't much traffic on the road.
What happened next, only Beryl knew?

Perhaps she was preoccupied, lost in a fog of deliberation, unhearing, unseeing, for whatever reason she failed to hear the rumbling - humming sound of the approaching vehicle. Suddenly and decisively she turned the stroller.

Abruptly startled Beryl sees the truck! - But it was too late.

The 27 year old driver, of the five-ton, grey Austin truck was unable to avoid hitting her.

As the heavy steel vehicle made contact, the truck struck the strollers wheel throwing Lorraine by the side of the road. The front mudguard hit the middle of Beryl's back knocking her off her feet. Throwing her into the air it sent her shoes flying landing some distance away, coming down hard she hit her head on the bitumen with an horrid thumping crack.

The truck on its way to Nowra was loaded with empty petrol drums. The driver put his foot on the brakes and came to a stop. The young male driver wearing thick-eye-glasses was in shock.

The driver and his passenger ran back to see the injured woman lying on her side unconscious, her head was bleeding. The child was near-by crying in the stroller. There was no-one around to help, so the truck driver drove down the road and stopped another car, asking them to go for help to the Falls Creek Post Office and phone for the Ambulance.

The wailing siren sound became louder as the Ambulance approached.

Joyce was still talking, when she was alerted something was wrong by the traffic, noticing that a car had stopped down the road.

Then adding to her curiosity the black and white Bedford Bus destined for Nowra had come to a stop. Still watching attentively Joyce said to her neighbour: "I wondered what the hold-up was.'

 Then suddenly the realization seized her and she yelled out loud "Oh...*my God*... Beryl's down there!"

Joyce's heart was pounding in her chest as she sprinted down the road. She was dreading what might have happened while fearful of what she might see.

Arriving at the scene she found Beryl pale and hurt, lying by the side of the road. Lorraine, who was close by was crying and covered with grime and gravel, one side of her face and arm was bleeding. The medic examined her and said she was OK.

Joyce said to son Beau: 'Go and find Skeet!' When Beau returned he said: "I couldn't find him, and I looked everywhere." Unbeknown to Joyce, someone had called in to see Skeet that morning asking him to help them with a 5 min job, and to have a few Christmas drinks.

Ambulance Officer Kelly was attending to Beryl while she lapsed in and out of consciousness, incoherently she murmured... mummy... mummy; before they loaded her into the back of the ambulance. Joyce was holding her hand and told her through tear-full-eyes "That it was going to be alright," but deep down she was fearful because Beryl didn't look too good.

The lights flashed and the siren wailed as the Ambulance drove northward along the Princes Hwy. To the left they passed the unfinished house named, *'Elimatta'* (Aboriginal word meaning 'my home'). To the right was the Jervis Bay turn-off, hastening on they reached the township of Nowra and the town's people stopped and stared.

The following information is from... the Inquisition before Coroner sitting alone.

Inquisition held at the Court House at Nowra in the state of NSW on the ninth day of January 1953 before Ulric Kerwick Walsh.

About 1:30pm: they arrived at the surgery in Nowra to see Dr Frances Ryan, his examination revealed Beryl had sustained large laceration associated with a known fracture of the cranium and occipital bone, along with multiple abrasions particularly of the lower limbs, with a spiral laceration on her left leg and bruises on her buttocks and back.

Beryl was then taken to the Shoalhaven District Memorial Hospital in Scenic Drive, upon arriving the medics stretchered her inside.

For a short while she responded to treatment. However at 4:15pm on that same afternoon, her condition deteriorated suddenly and she died half an hour later. The cause of the death was profound shock, associated with a known fracture of the skull

Beryl was in God's hands now.

At about 6:30pm at the Mortuary of the Memorial Hospital Nowra; Julie Rigby a nursing assistant at the Hospital identified Beryl's body to the Coroner Ulric Kerwick Walsh and (1st class) Constable Barkwith. She said:

> "The deceased was well known to me, she lived
> near my parents' home at Falls Creek."

Skeet, upon returning to his sister's place was told what had happened, and went to the hospital, to identify his wife. The Police were there, and he recognized Mr Green's step-daughter sixteen year old Julie Rigby.

Beryl was just lying there and he couldn't see her breathing, yet he wasn't ready to accept it, and had to ask. They told him, that yes, she had definitely died.

With regrets one after another running through his head, Skeet returned home with Joyce, he was wound up tighter than a two bob watch, when his blonde headed nephew, eight year old Beau, showing deep concern in his large blue eyes said: "Uncle Skeet how's Aunty Bev?" With a callous tone Skeet snapped at Beau saying: *"Don't"*...Call me Skeet! *The Names REG!* Then quietly told him: *"She had died"*... It was a day Beau never forgot.

The Police knocked on the door of 6 Staff Street, delivering the bad news. Topsy was speechless, as she tried to absorb what had happened.

At Berala; Dot was near the phone when it rang in the hallway; her daughter Barbara was watching while her mother answer the phone wondering who was calling and what was being said, because her mother's face was reflecting the pain of the awful news. Shaken... Dot slowly replaced the receiver while struggling to overcome what had happened.

The News in the papers wrote; -

Women Killed by Lorry 16/12/51

NOWRA Monday Mrs Beryl Rae, 25 of Falls Creek, near Nowra, was hit by a lorry on Princes Highway, at Falls Creek, this afternoon, she died from injuries.

The police were told she was pushing a two year old child in a stroller and was crossing the highway diagonally when hit by the lorry which was driven by a man from Milton.

She was taken to the Shoalhaven District Memorial Hospital by the Shoalhaven Ambulance, and was admitted with a fractured skull from which she died later, the child was unhurt.

Chapter 25

The Funeral

Beryl's mum and Eileen made all the arrangements for the funeral and Reg (Skeet) was glad those people were there to help him because he was hopeless at the time. He didn't know what was going on. He had lost his wife and the feelings of aloneness were overwhelming - besides the responsibilities of looking after his daughter and he wasn't ready for any of it.

The notice was sent to the Sydney Morning Herald

RAE - The Relatives and Friends of the Family of the late Mrs BERYL WINSOME RAE of Falls Creek, via Nowra, are kindly invited to attend her Funeral, which is to leave A.S/Cole's Funeral Parlours, Wollongong, This Wednesday after service at 1.30 p.m. for the Woronora Crematorium A.S. COLE. Funeral Director, Telephone B3024, Wollongong.

Two days later...Wednesday 17th December 1952,
Wollongong Woronora Crematorium, 1:30pm.

With barely enough time to accept what had happened Reg, Lorraine, Joyce and Bert arrived at the Chapel joining the sorrowful family and friends Reg was bearing up all right, or so he thought. Topsy, John, Dot and Bill, arrived in a hired car, and not far behind came the hearse.

The atmosphere was intense it was charged with the anxiety felt in each person's grieving heart, adding to the despair Lorraine couldn't be comforted and wouldn't stop crying for her mother. She just didn't understand what had happened; all she knew was that life was different now. The solid ground she once stood on with her mother's love was gone and her life was in chaos.

The congregation listened to the account of her inspiringly short life; one that was filled with challenges right from the start. How she had a lot of difficulties and sadness in her early life and how she had risen to meet each challenge with courage and won.

Annie had lost a daughter, Dot and Bob their sister, Reg his wife and Lorraine had lost her mother.

-Ecclesiastes 3. 1-8
A time to be born, a time to die,
A time to plant, a time to reap,
A time to kill, a time to heal,
A time to laugh, a time to weep.
A time to build up, a time to break down,
A time to dance, a time to mourn,.

When the funeral service had ended and the final curtain was drawn without speaking Reg left the family and went outside. Sitting alone on the top step he was feeling numb, while fumbling with the blue box of Federal matches he tried to light-up a smoke. Through glazed eyes he was remembering her face, and the things she said - while if only thoughts were running through his head. Up until then he thought he had it under control. There wasn't a tear or anything but he wasn't talking either.

Seeing her dad - Lorraine ran over to him putting her arm around his shoulders her eyes widened, when he suddenly grabbed her and held her tight and that's when he broke down and couldn't stop crying.

It really hurt - he was a broken man after that.

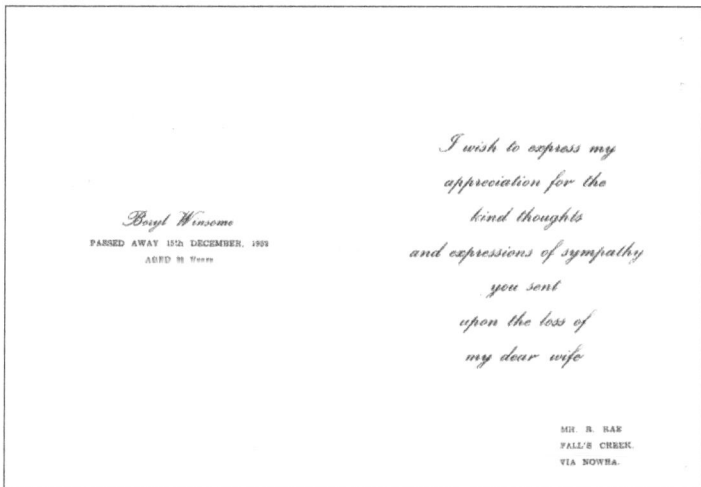

With Sincere Thanks
I wish to express my appreciation for the kind thoughts and expressions of sympathy you sent upon the loss of my dear wife.
Mr R. Rae

The Lost Letter

Creating more stress for Tospy after the funeral, the lost Air-Mail letter from Beryl arrived in her mother's post box.

The faded blue Air-Mail letter beared the story of its journey, a red line drawn on one side a large blue circle on the other side, stamped three times... undeliverable, stamped return to sender, then stamped T...18D...Centimes. (I know how she must have felt reading that letter, because I was overwhelmed when I read it over 50 years later.)

The whole family was upset crying out how it was so unfair - after all she had been through - why Beryl?

But now they were angry and wanted to know what happened! On the 9th January 1953; just three weeks after the funeral there was an inquest held at the Court House in Nowra.

The District Coroner, Mr U. K. Walsh, J.P who inquired into the cause of death of Beryl Winsome Rae, of Falls Creek, on the December 15, 1952, after being struck by a motor lorry, returned a verdict of accidental death.

According to the evidence given at the inquest, Sidney Alexander Mathie, the driver of the lorry, was proceeding from Milton to Nowra on the day mentioned, he was travelling at a speed of approximately 30 mph, about nine miles from Nowra, when he noticed the deceased walking in the same direction pushing a stroller. She was walking on the bitumen about three feet from the edge of the bitumen when the Lorry was about 60 to 70 yards from the women. She suddenly turned to her right to cross the road.

The driver of the lorry reduced speed to pass her, and when almost level with her, she suddenly swung round to her left into the path of the Lorry. The driver pulled the lorry hard to his right to avoid striking her, but the front near side mudguard struck the women.

Mathie: immediately stopped his vehicle and his passenger, a woman from Milton Mrs Petty did what she could to assist the women and child until the Shoalhaven District Ambulance arrived and conveyed her to the Nowra District Memorial Hospital, were according to Dr. J.F.Ryan's evidence, she died a few hours later from profound shock associated with a fracture of the skull.

According to the evidence of Mrs Petty of Milton, immediately after the accident the stroller was standing on the gravel shoulder of the road, about two feet from the edge of the bitumen, on the western side of the road.

In reply to a question by the Coroner, Mrs Petty said: "The child was in the stroller after the impact." To Snr. Const. Hale (for the Police) she said the driver had slowed down to about 10 mph when about the length of the court room from where deceased was walking.

Evidence showed that only one wheel of the stroller was damaged by the impact, the baby was not thrown out of the stroller and was not hurt in any way.

Mr K. C. F. Harris, of Morton and Harris, appeared to watch the interests of the insurance company and of the driver of the lorry, Sidney Alexander Mathie. Mr T. B. McInerney, of Maguire and McInerney, of Wollongong, watched the interests of the relatives of the deceased; and W. G. Hale conducted the case for the police.

An inquest, held on 9th Jan 1953, finding it was accidental no blame was given to the driver 27 year old Sidney Mathie.[27]

The Shoal haven and Nowra News Jan 13, 1953- Report:

The Sydney Morning Herald
RAE, Beryl Winsome.-(nee Wyber) December 15, 1952. Result of accident, late of Prince's Highway, Falls Creek, via Nowra, beloved daughter and step-daughter of Mr and Mrs, John Burkhardt, of Wollongong dear wife of Reginald, and mother of Lorraine, and sister of William of Gwyneville, Robert of England and Dorothy of Berala aged 25 years.

_____

The Sydney Morning Herald Tuesday 15th Dec 1953
RAE.- Treasured memories of our darling daughter, Beryl (nee Wyber. Result of accident, aged 25 years, December 15, 1952. May the sunshine she missed on life's highway, be found in God's haven of rest, sadly missed by mum and step-father.

_____

The Sydney Morning Herald
RAE. - In loving memory of dear Beryl, who passed away December 15th, 1952 Always remember by Nana Roden, and Aunty Ruth, Uncle George.

_____
_____

27

After the devastating loss of his wife, my father (Reg) was all twisted at the time when he decided to go to Tasmania. That was after his mother had told him to get away from the area (Falls Creek, NSW.) he stayed with his brother Bill & his wife in Launceston working in the Dry Cleaners. In 1954 he found a job in Burnie working for Nor-West Cleaners at 12 Mount St and boarded at the "Summerset Hotel."

Reg had also worked at the Wynyard branch for two and half years.

1956 he was employed as a despatch loader at the Tasmanian Board Mills Limited, but it didn't last long because the Mill was shutting down.

After work he would go to the Wynyard Hotel meeting new people and trying to forget the past.

But always in the back of his mind he had to get back to see his daughter Lorraine, to see if she was alright. Lorraine was living at Blackwall Mountain near Woy Woy, NSW with his elderly parents, or as he had hoped to build a place in Tasmania, however his elderly parents said it was too cold for them to live in Tasmania. So he went back to Woy Woy to live, but he was never happy there and always longed to go back to Tasmania to live.

Epilogue

My first memories were of being moved around from one relative to another, then living at 13 Springwood Ave, Blackwall Mountain near Woy Woy with my grandparents, Nan (Eileen) in her mid-sixties and Par (Bill), in his mid-seventies. Yes Eileen's prophecy did come true, she would have to look after Beryl's children if she died or in this case her only child, me. But in the end it was her-own-free will that it ended up that way.

The one bedroom home, painted white, with a skillion roof, had a set of two windows at the front. It was sparsely furnished with a green vinyl settee in the lounge room was where I slept. In the morning the bedclothes were folded away again.

It was situated next to Nan and Pars bedroom, which had a built in wardrobe with a curtain drawn in front. On the top shelf are were the memories of my mother's life are kept, a diary, two photo albums, a shoe-box containing wedding trinkets, satin horse shoe, engagement ring, and a purple coloured velvet ring box, holding the wedding ring..

It's been six decades since that fateful day; Dad said:

'She wanted to be as good as everyone else, that she was better than most, you just don't meet them like her now, there was no anger no hate, and we could always sit down talk it over no matter what the problem was.'

This was the start of my journey - I have gone on to become a stronger person learning to cope with my own struggles and stresses. I have learnt many things that nothing is perfect and forgiveness is strength. I have learnt that carrying the past into the future is like wearing too many overcoats it's too heavy a burden to carry.

At the same time, I haven't forgotten the lessons and have learnt from them.

The scent of a rose can't be seen but you know it exits.

It took some time before I understood that spine tingling moments, when the hairs on the back of your neck stand on end the goose bumps on your arms; finally I understood that her guiding spirit had never really left me.

The Wall of Memories holds my mother's ashes, I realize death is just another path, the journey that we all must take and I take some comfort in knowing that one day we will be together in the end.

Woronora Gardens Panel 23 Sutherland

211

References

Children- Collaroy. [Online Video]. 1940. Available from: http://aso.gov.au/titles/home-movies/homes-for-crippled-children/clip2/. [Accessed: 17/1/12].

'Funereal Notice', *Sydney Morning Herald*, 15th December 1953, page 264

Hamilton, D.G, 1979. Hand in Hand the story of the Royal Alexandra Hospital for Children. 1st ed. Sydney: John Ferguson.

National Film and Sound Archive. (1929). Here comes Santa. [Online Video]. 1929. Available from: http://aso.gov.au/titles/ads/here-comes-santa/clip3/. [Accessed: 17/1/12].

National Film and Sound Archive. (1940). Homes for Crippled 'Santa visiting the Royal Alexandra Hospital', *Sydney Morning Herald*, 23rd November 1929, page 21.

Simpson, M. 'Lessons in bed', *Sydney Morning Herald*, 14th January 1954, page 48.

Sydney Morning Herald, 1st February 1952, page 3

The Society for Crippled Children established in 1929

'William's son William', *The Brisbane Courier*, 25th August 1932, page 20.

'Woman Killed by Lorry', Shoalhaven &Nowra News, 16th December 1952

Woods, J. Big Girls Don't Cry (more details neded)

Deborah Mason | Acting Deputy Registrar/Assistant Coroner | Courts Services | Department of Justice and Attorney General Nowra Court House, Plunkett Street, Nowra NSW 2541 | PO Box 579, Nowra NSW 2541

Heaven's Special Mum

www.ingramcontent.com/pod-product-compliance
Lightning Source LLC
Chambersburg PA
CBHW030924090426
42737CB00007B/316